the
ACCURATE
ROUTER

the
ACCURATE
ROUTER

Quick Setups and Simple Jigs

Ian Kirby

CAMBIUM PRESS

Newtown

The Accurate Router

ISBN 0-9643999-7-0

First printing: November 1998
Printed in the United States of America

Published by
    Cambium Press
    PO Box 909
    Bethel, CT 06801
    tel 203-426-6481 fax 203-426-0722
    email CAMBIUMBOOKS.COM

Distributed to the book trade by
    Lyons Press
    123 W 18th St, 6th Flr
    New York NY 10011
    tel 212-620-9580 fax 212-929-1836

**Library of Congress
Cataloging-in-Publication Data**
Kirby, Ian J., 1932-
    The accurate router : quick setups and
simple jigs / by Ian J. Kirby.
        p.   cm.
    Includes index.
    ISBN 0-9643999-7-0 (alk. paper)
    1. Routers (Tools)   I. Title
TT186.K573   1998
684'.083--dc21   98-37568
                                        CIP

Contents

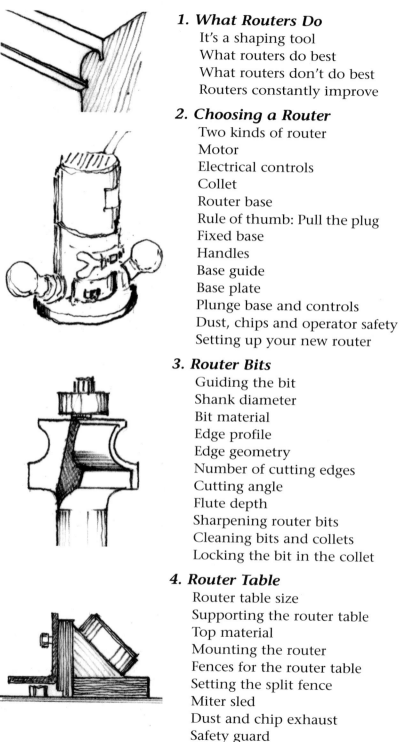

Contents

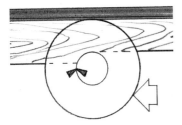

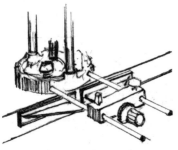

Contents

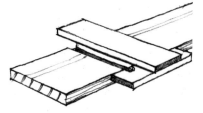

Contents

Author's introduction

Imagine a sharp and new carbide-tipped router bit cutting through wood — like a knife through water. It's efficient, it's clean, it's almost effortless. That's what you bought when you invested in your router, that incredible cutting ability.

However, when they told you about the many and wondrous things this tool will do, they lied.

It won't do any of them.

It cuts wood, that's what it does.

You do all the rest.

"The rest" consists of choosing the right bit for the job at hand, starting and stopping in the right place, and steering the right line in between. That about sums up cutting wood.

You will get three things from this book: how to choose your equipment, how to hold the work still, and how to guide the router along the path you want it to take.

It's as simple and as sophisticated as the way someone once described baseball to me. You throw the ball, you hit the ball, you catch the ball — and sometimes it rains. So play a great game and have a good time doing it.

> Ian Kirby
>
> Milford, CT
>
> October 1998

Acknowledgments

For their support with tools and equipment, my gratitude and thanks to:

Dick Redpath of Dewalt Industrial Tool Co.

Brad Witt of Woodhaven, Durant, Iowa

Peter Hopkins of Porter Cable

David Kellar of Kallar & Co., Petaluma, CA

Eric Savelle of Tools Plus, Waterbury, CT

Richard Wedler of Microfence, Hollywood, CA

Crisp, elegant moldings and panels can be run on the router table.

Chapter One

What Routers Do

The portable electric router has changed woodworking. It is the most versatile tool ever invented. With modern bits, it can make clean, tear-free cuts. It is fast, and it does not require a lot of skill to operate — in fact, making accurate jigs to guide the router requires more skill than completing the actual routing.

As a consequence the marketplace is awash with accessories and gadgets manufactured for the router. There are dozens of mail-order catalogs, magazines, and books devoted to woodworking with the router and to the gadgets that go with it. Why, then, would anyone write another router book?

One answer is that for all the noise and ink, there was no comprehensive handbook that enumerates and analyzes the seven basic ways of guiding the router. While other router handbooks present a lot of useful techniques, none offers a systematic approach that helps the woodworker decide how best to proceed. This handbook fills the void.

Elegant tusk-tenon joints feature routed double mortises and tenons.

Three-way showcase joint, also shown on the front cover, is mitered and connected with a loose tenon in matching routed slots. More on page 113.

Another answer is that other router books and magazine articles advocate needless complexity. They advise woodworkers to make or buy elaborate jigs and fixtures in order to accomplish simple tasks. Making the jig is likely to take longer and cost more than the woodworking project — jig-making itself becomes the objective, not woodworking. Paralysis can be the result of following that path. This handbook shows you how to use blocks and clamps to make simple, single-purpose jigs and fixtures. This approach is quick, cheap, and versatile. You can get on with your woodworking project.

The router's strong suit is its potential for truly accurate work. The machine's shaft and collet whirl the cutter in near-perfect rotation, the base drops the cutter to precise depth, the machine or the workpiece moves smoothly along a guided path. What could possibly go wrong? Yet as all amateur woodworkers know, it isn't quite that easy. A million little events occur between the desire for a perfect cut and the actual achievement of it. This book shows you how to steer between the rocks and achieve the superbly accurate results you're looking for.

It's a shaping tool

The router is a shaping tool and a finishing tool. Whether you want to make toys, furniture, decorative objects, boats, or trim for your house, the router is an essential part of your tool kit. It can help you cut parts to the shape and size you want, make joints that fit, and shape the design details your project requires.

However, for all its versatility, the router is not a universal woodworking machine. Successful woodworking is a chain of events, and if the only tool you have is a router, you won't be able to complete any projects. This is because the router is not a breakdown tool. It's of extremely limited value for roughing the wood you want out of large planks and sheets, and it's not able to bring a plank of wood to precise finished dimensions. It's best to think of the router as one important tool among many, and to use it for the shaping, joint making, detailing, and finishing operations it does best. Turn elsewhere when you come up against the router's limitations.

What routers do best

Here are some of the operations routers do best. Of course you can combine any of these operations to achieve the results you want.

Page 133

Page 135

Page 142

—Cut a straight, smooth edge on a piece of wood. This allows you to join wood edge-to-edge, to make wide pieces out of narrow ones. (See page 129.)

—Trim solid wood lippings for plywood, particle board, and MDF, for use with plastic laminates and veneers. (See page 132.)

—Cut circles and ellipses in wood. This allows you to make wheels, tabletops, frames, and other highly regulated parts. (See page 131.)

—Cut rebates on the edge of the wood. This allows you to make frames for pictures or panels, and doors that fit their openings. (See page 135.)

—Cut a series of rebates to produce precise tenons and other joint-making elements, to construct sturdy and attractive furniture and built-ins. (See page 142.)

—Cut grooves and dadoes on the edge or face of the wood. (Grooves run with the wood grain, dadoes or housings run across the wood grain.) This allows you to join one piece of wood to another, to make boxes, and to put shelves in cabinets. (See page 137.)

—Cut a complex shape in the edge of a piece of wood. This allows you to make moldings, and also to rout decorative profiles on the edges of doors and tops for tables and cabinets. (See page 133.)

Page 141

Page 144

Page 147

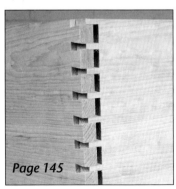

Page 145

—Drill precise holes in wood. This allows you to make strong dowel joints, as well as to create interesting decorative effects. (See page 144.)

—Cut a deep and precise recess in the middle of a piece of wood. This allows you to make mortises for mortise-and-tenon joints. (See page 142.)

—Cut a piece of wood the exact size and shape of a jig or master pattern. This allows you to make multiple pieces of wood, such as parts for chair legs and arms, that are all the same size and shape. (See page 143.)

—With the aid of a jig, cut the complex shape of a dovetail joint for making boxes and drawers. (See page 145.)

—Follow a pattern to cut a shallow recess in the surface of a piece of wood. This allows you to rout letters and other decorative shapes in the wood. (See page 80.)

—Follow a pattern to cut a shape out of one piece of wood, and a perfectly matching hole in another piece. This allows you to inlay one piece of wood into another. (See page 80.)

—Make a flat surface on an otherwise unworkable piece of wood, such as a burl or section through a tree trunk. (See page 132.)

—Follow a pattern to make a two-dimensional or three-dimensional shape in the wood. This allows you to make curved panels for furniture and sculpture. (See page 123.)

What routers don't do best

For all their versatility, there are many essential woodworking operations that routers can be forced to do, but do not do very well. These operations are all necessary for breaking the wood you want out of planks and sheets, and for preparing the wood for subsequent operations. Here are some examples of things that routers might be forced to accomplish, but cannot do well.

—Harvest project parts from large planks of solid wood or sheets of man-made material. The tool of choice is the handsaw, the skilsaw, or the portable jigsaw.

—Put a truly flat surface on a piece of wood (that is, create a face side). It's possible to surface rough wood with a router, but it requires a jig (page 132), it's extremely slow and tedious, and it makes a righteous mess of tiny chips. The correct tool is the jointer or the hand plane.

—Plane the other surface of the wood parallel to its face side. As when creating the face side in the first place, you can do it with the router but it is difficult, tedious, and messy. Use the thickness planer or hand planes instead.

—Put a truly square edge on a piece of wood (that is, create the face edge). The tool of choice is the jointer or hand planes. The router will do the job once you have made a face side, but since you needed a jointer to create the face side in the first place, why not use the jointer to prepare the face edge as well?

—Crosscut wood square and to precise length. The tools of choice are the chopsaw or the table saw.

—Rip wood to precise width. The tool of choice is the tablesaw; you can also use the bandsaw, skilsaw or portable jigsaw.

The table saw is a breakdown tool, while the router is a finishing tool. The two machines work very well together.

Routers constantly improve

People like to think of woodworking as a set of traditional tools and techniques that don't change. In fact, woodworking tools and techniques are always evolving, and at times they evolve extremely rapidly. I like the old story about the woodworker who is being scolded for giving up molding planes in favor of an electric router. He is told, "Surely that's not how your grandfather would have done it." The woodworker replies, "Well, he was a darned smart fella, so if he could have had a router like mine, he'd have done just what I'm doing." Then he flips the switch to drown out any more antiquated nonsense.

Routers first appeared early in this century. Since about 1940, there has been constant improvement. The important innovations include:

—**Motor units**. Reliable, high-speed motor units that wind up toward 18,000 RPM under load. Such speeds allow the cutter to take such a tiny bite each time it goes around that even the hardest and most difficult materials will yield. (See page 20.)

Electrical controls

Fixed and plunge

—**Electrical controls**. Router motors now come with much improved start mechanisms and speed controls. It's possible to buy a soft-start motor that won't kick itself out of position when you turn it on, with a precise speed control that can either be pre-set for particular operations, or adjusted on the fly to achieve optimum results (see page 21).

—**Fixed and plunge**. Originally, routers had a fixed base, which made them excellent for machining edges but not so good for starting or ending a cut in the middle of the edge or on the face of the workpiece. Now you can buy a plunge router, which allows you to position the tool, start the motor, and then lower the cutter into the workpiece. Even better, several manufacturers have standardized their mid-sized routers on a motor unit that is 3.5 inches in diameter. These motors will fit a variety of fixed and plunge bases (see page 24).

Collets

Bits

Jigs and accessories

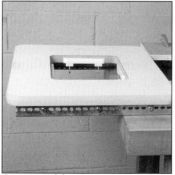
Router table

—Collet. Collet design and manufacture has improved. Since the collet is the part that connects the router cutter to the motor, it's critical that it not only gets a good grip and does not slip, but also that it release the bit without an argument when you want to change to a different operation. Modern collets are reliable and safe, provided they're kept clean and have not been damaged by rough handling. (See page 22.)

—Bits. There are hundreds of router bits on the market. Bit design is constantly being improved by new materials and by the addition of special profiles. At the same time, it's still true that a small kit of standard profiles will handle most of the practical routing that most woodworkers need to do. You don't have to make a huge investment in bits to get a lot out of your router. (See page 34.)

—Jigs and accessories. There's now a huge array of router jigs and accessories in the marketplace. Standard accessories that most router owners should consider include specialized fences, template guides, base plates, and jigs for making dovetails and other woodworking joints. Although some accessories are better than others, most of them contain a design idea that's worth ferreting out so you can use it for yourself.

—Router table. A router table secures the machine in one position, so you can move the workpiece past the cutter. In many situations this approach is both more accurate and more versatile. Woodworkers have always been able to design and build their own router tables, but now you can buy parts to build a table to suit your needs at less expense than trying to make every component yourself. (See page 48.)

—Chips and mess. By its nature, the router throws chips and makes a lot of mess. But you can get it under control with modern shop vacuums and dust-control systems. (See page 55.)

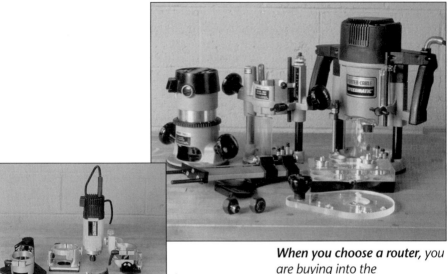

When you choose a router, you are buying into the manufacturer's system.

Chapter Two
Choosing a Router

Spending a lot of time trying to figure out which router will be best to buy is futile. In fact there is no absolute best, there are only choices and trade-offs.

The first thing to know is that as with other kinds of machinery, you generally do get what you pay for. You can find sale prices and promotional bargains, but you can't expect the cheapest machine to be the best machine. Conversely, when you find yourself considering several machines from reputable manufacturers, you can expect comparably priced units to be of comparable quality.

The second thing to know is that no single router can possibly be the best for every kind of work. Whatever you choose as a starting point, it won't be long before you own more than one router.

The third thing is that when you choose a router, you are buying into a manufacturer's system. While bits are interchangeable from router to router, many accessories are not interchangeable. Consequently, in order to choose between two equally acceptable machines, you need to examine each manufacturer's complete product line.

Fixed-base router

Plunge router

Two kinds of router

There are two basic types of router:

Fixed base router,

Plunge router.

All routers consist of two basic parts.

Motor,

Base.

The motor has three elements:

Power unit,

ON-OFF **switch** and other electrical controls,

Tapered socket in the armature, which holds the collet.

The base has five elements:

Base casting, which includes the height adjustment for the motor,

Locking device to hold the height setting,

Handles,

Mounting holes for fences, base guides, and trammels,

Base plate, which accepts guide collars.

All routers consist of a motor and a base.

Motor

The motor powers the router. All router motors have universal windings, which means that in the absence of a load, they crank up toward infinitely high speeds. Friction and inertia impose a practical speed limit around 23,000 RPM under load, most routers operate between 16,000 RPM and 18,000 RPM, depending on the wood being cut.

Routers are often marketed by motor horsepower, but manufacturers' ratings include a shinola factor. Current draw, or amperage, gives you a more useful comparison:

Under 3/4 HP (5 amps), laminate trimmers and detail routers;

3/4 HP to 2 HP (5 amps to 15 amps), mid-size, general purpose routers;

2 HP and up (over 15 amps), large routers.

Although these designations help compare machines, small differences between similar routers don't really matter. This is because the operator can adjust the load on the motor in three ways:

Change the volume of the cut by moving the fence or changing the depth setting,

Replace a dull cutter with a sharp one,

Change the feed speed.

Three sizes: laminate trimmer, general-purpose router, large plunge router

Electrical controls

All routers have an ON-OFF **switch**. In most fixed-base machines, the switch is built into the top of the motor housing. Most plunge routers cable the switch into the handles. You can start and stop these machines without letting go.

When choosing a router, it's important to make sure the ON-OFF switch is located where your fingers can find it, without you having to look or to let go of the handles. If the switch location doesn't work for you, or if it seems to flip the wrong way, you may be considering the wrong router. Once you have chosen a router, spend the time it takes to become instinctive about hitting that switch in a millisecond.

A recent addition to plunge-router control systems is **electronic speed control**. Makers vary in how they mark the speed setting — some give RPMs, while others assign an arbitrary number. There's no advantage either way.

Variable speed is particularly important with large routers that have the power to swing large cutters. Most variable speed control units not only allow you to set the speed to match the cutter diameter, they also maintain the set speed under varying load conditions.

Speed controls

Most variable speed systems include a soft start feature. When you hit the on switch, the cutter gradually ramps up to full speed. This eliminates the kick that otherwise comes with the instant application of full current.

Manufacturers match electrical controls to the motor. If you buy after-market controls, like variable speed boxes or foot switches, be sure their electrical capacity (in watts, or volts multiplied by amps) matches or exceeds that of the router's motor.

ON-OFF switch styles

Collet

The collet is the metal socket that connects the router bit to the end of the motor shaft. Manufacturers' designs vary, but the objective is always the same: grip the shank of the bit or cutter without slipping and spin it concentrically without any wobble.

On a well-engineered router, the collet is a three-part assembly:

Tapered hole in the end of the motor shaft,

Collet,

Lock nut.

In strict machine-shop terms, the **tapered hole** is the collet, but in the world of routers the word means the sleeve that fits inside the tapered hole. Each manufacturer chooses its own taper angle, so you can't expect to swap the collet from one manufacturer to a different make of router.

Collets. Some designs separate into sleeve and lock nut, while other designs lock together with a circlip or an internal press fit. Collets are not interchangeable from one manufacturer to another.

The outside of the motor shaft is threaded to accept the **lock nut**, which pulls the tapered collet into the tapered hole, thereby tightening it around the cutter shank. As with the tapered sleeve, you can't interchange lock nuts from one manufacturer to another. This means that while you can mix your router bits, you can't mix collets. Once you have routers from more than one manufacturer, you have to organize the collet parts and wrenches accordingly.

The **collet** has an outer wall tapered to conform exactly to the tapered hole in the motor shaft. The collet's inside wall is a cylinder the size of the bit shank. However, in order to grip the bit shank, the collet must somehow be made flexible. The simplest way to achieve flexibility is to cut a slit through the collet wall. More sophisticated and more flexible collets have four or six slits.

Collet size, which corresponds to the diameter of the bit shank, is another way of designating router size. There are three collet sizes in common use:

1/4 inch (6mm),

3/8 inch (9mm),

1/2 inch (12mm).

Most trim routers accept only the small 1/4-inch (6mm) collet. Medium-sized and large routers usually have interchangeable collets or collet adapters, so they can accept bits with 1/4-inch (6mm) and 1/2-inch (12mm) shanks. Manufacturers stopped making 3/8-inch (9mm) shank bits some years ago, but 3/8-inch (9mm) collet adapters are still available for most machines.

PARTS OF THE COLLET

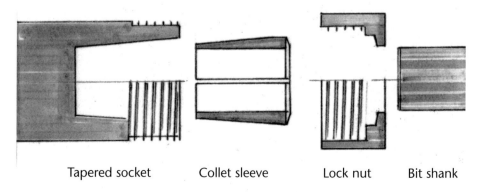

Tapered socket   Collet sleeve   Lock nut   Bit shank

Router base

The router base is an aluminum casting with handles. It connects the operator to the machine. It also houses the up-down mechanism for raising and lowering the cutter. The design of the base separates the two styles of machine:

Fixed-base router,

Plunge router.

You can use either type of router above the workpiece or in the router table. However, fixed-base routers are better suited to router tables, because they have positive height adjustment mechanisms. Most plunge routers have to come out of the table to be adjusted, though there are some aftermarket devices that let you fine-tune the depth of cut with the router in place. Note that laminate trimmers and other small routers always have a fixed base.

Fixed-base router   *Plunge router*

Rule of thumbscrew: Pull the plug

Before you attempt to change cutters or adjust the cutting depth of a fixed-base router, you must pull the electrical plug. The on-off switch probably has some kind of a safety shroud or interlock, but Murphy's Law means you can't rely on it. Unimaginable things can go wrong while you wrestle with the depth setting, with fingers and wrenches stuck in the mechanism.

Take no chances. Pull the plug.

Fixed base

The fixed base holds the motor and has some form of thumbscrew that tightens the base around the motor. You have to release the thumbscrew to raise or lower the motor in its housing, thereby adjusting the depth of cut.

There are three common methods for adjusting depth of cut:

Spiral groove and pin,

Spiral ramp and buttress,

Rack and pinion.

All three designs are effective systems that permit fine adjustments. The **spiral-groove** and **spiral-ramp** designs engage a pin or block. You adjust the mechanism by rotating the motor in the base, then you lock the setting with a wing-nut or thumbscrew. The **rack and pinion** design has a small gear that engages a straight track.

If you plan to use the router underneath a table, consider how easy it will be to adjust the height without dismantling the setup. Rack-and-pinion and spiral-groove systems hold the motor in the base when upside down, but the ramp-and-buttress design does not. You have to hold the motor when you loosen the screw, or else it drops to the floor.

Fixed-base height adjustments: The spiral-groove-and-pin router, top left, and spiral-ramp-and-buttress router, left, adjust by rotating the motor in the base casting. The rack-and-pinion router, above, has a calibrated dial and adjusts straight up and down.

Handles

Fixed-base routers have two knobs or handles for the operator to grasp. The lower the handles, the easier it will be to control the router. Some manufacturers also offer pistol grips or a single D-handle, with the ON-OFF switch mounted in the handle. Whatever the handle style, be sure it's comfortable for you, and that you can reach the ON-OFF switch without losing control of the router.

Handle styles: round knobs, pistol grip, and D-handle. The pistol grip and D-handle have trigger-style ON-OFF switches.

Base guide

DeWalt and Elu base guide has a lead screw for fine adjustments.

Microfence base guide, shown mounted on a Porter-Cable router, is a precision instrument.

Most router base castings have two horizontal holes machined into them, to accept a base guide. Two rods on the base guide run through these holes and can be locked in place with thumbscrews.

Newer edge guides, and the excellent Microfence after-market system (shown below), offer lead-screw adjustability. They're a big improvement over old-style guesswork guides.

Router literature often calls the base guide a "fence," but it is an extension of the router base, not a fence. It bears against and is guided by the edge of the work-piece, which plays the role of fence in the setup.

The relationship between the base guide and the router handles is important for stability. The router in the top photo has handles in line with the base-guide mounting rods, which puts the handles at right angles to the base guide itself. This puts one handle firmly on top of the workpiece in near-ly every routing situation. The router in the bottom photo has handles that line up with the base guide. It will be very tippy and unsta-ble whenever you are using the guide to shape the edge of the workpiece.

Base plate

On the bottom of the metal base casting is screwed a base plate. It's usually a black phenolic or acrylic disk about 3/16 inch thick. The base plate has three roles:

Its edge is the router's **guide surface**,

It accepts **guide collars** for template routing.

It is the **smooth face** on which the router rides,

When you drive the router against a fence, the **guide surface** of the base plate is what actually makes contact. The base plate has to pass easily over the wood, so check that it has no burrs or sharp edges. If it does, sand it smooth with 600-grit paper.

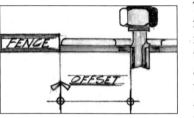

The distance from the base plate's **guide surface** to the edge of the bit's cutting circle, normally about 2-1/2 inches (6cm), is called the **offset** (see page 69). If the guide edge of a circular base plate isn't exactly concentric with the cutter, the offset will change according to exactly how you position the router. If you make a second cut with a different part of the base plate touching the fence, the cut will shift. For this reason, some manufacturers oversize the base plate screw holes, and chamfer the collet nut, so it's possible to center the base plate.

Most base plates have a rebate around the center hole in which you can fit **guide collars**. The outer rim of the collar bears against a template or fence, thus becoming the router's guide surface. The offset becomes the distance from the outside of the collar to the cutter. Guide collars come in various sizes. Most manufacturers make their own guide collars, but some makes also accept standard aftermarket collars.

Chamfered lock nut helps center the base plate.

Guide collars screw into the rebated center hole in the router base plate.

Aftermarket base plates

Every manufacturer sells spare base plates, and every after-market router outfit offers its own base plates. They're readily obtainable and they aren't expensive. If you need an odd-shaped plate, chances are you'll be able to find what you need. Two aftermarket base plates that most woodworkers will be able to use are:

Oversized, rectangular base plate,

Offset base plate.

Oversized rectangular base plates made of 3/8-inch phenolic or Lexan commonly are used to retain a router upside-down in the router table. This kind of plate also solves the problem of concentricity, because you can't rotate it to a new position. It's a good general purpose alternative to the standard round plate.

The **offset base plate** helps stabilize the router when you are using a pilot bearing bit or when you are molding an edge. In these situations more than half of the router base hangs unsupported off the workpiece. The offset base puts more of the base back onto the workpiece.

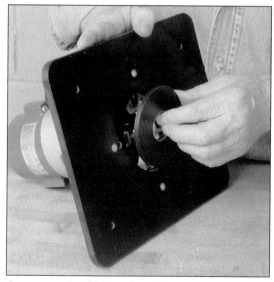

Some oversized base plates have interchangeable center inserts to accommodate different sized router bits.

The offset base plate, which replaces the standard plate, helps stabilize the router. However, some offset bases interfere with the base guide, so they can't be used together.

Plunge base and controls

Unlike a fixed-base router, a plunge router allows you to move the motor up and down while it is running. Working between guides and stops, it's easy to position the router on the workpiece, then lower the cutter into the wood. You can start and stop the cut in the middle of the workpiece.

The plunge router motor slides up and down on two spring-loaded steel columns. The plunge mechanism typically includes a screw for setting the depth of cut, one or more stops for retaining depth settings, and a lock for stopping and releasing the plunge mechanism.

Plunge motor and collet

Most plunge routers are 2 HP or larger, and most recent models include a variable speed control and soft-start electronics. The collet assembly isn't any different from the one found on a fixed-base router.

Plunge handles and switches

The handle style and the position of the controls on plunge routers differ from fixed-base routers. The plunge action means the handles may start out high, but once plunged you want the handles to be as low and close to the workpiece as possible. And you must be able to reach and operate the plunge lock lever, as well as the ON-OFF switch, without fumbling or guessing.

The amount of effort it takes to plunge the router varies from one brand to another. This is one of the things to try before buying.

Plunge router handle styles and control layouts

Plunge depth stop

The depth stop mechanism limits the router's downward plunge. The details of the mechanism vary among manufacturers, but most have an adjustable rod that stops against a turret. The turret, which may have three, four, or six positions, allows you to approach full depth in stages. It also permits setting more than one working depth.

Depth stop

Plunge return

The plunge return is a double nut on a threaded rod that limits the machine's upward travel. In the router table, it can be used as a depth adjustment. Aftermarket coupling devices are available to improve its accessibility.

Plunge lock lever

The plunge lock lever stops and releases the router's plunge mechanism. It's usually on the left side of the router, and it should be in easy reach, because you need to lock and release the mechanism without letting go of the router handles. The design of the plunge lock lever varies widely among manufacturers. Some release the plunge when activated and some lock it, some flip up and some flip down, some are easy to toggle and some take an effort. You just have to try various brands to find out which mechanism works best for you.

Plunge return

Plunge lock levers vary widely from one manufacturer to the next. Try them all to see which feels most natural to you.

Dust, chips, and operator safety

Wood chips expand to three or more times the volume of the original wood. The router's high speed throws the chips all over the room. Chips and dust from MDF and other man-made materials are especially nasty — you really don't want to breathe this stuff, nor get it in your eyes.

Goggles protect your eyesight

Before you switch on the router, and every time you switch it on, be sure you are wearing safety glasses. Every hardware store and home center sells plastic goggles that surround your eyes. Most goggles are large enough to contain regular 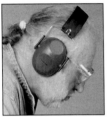 eyeglasses. As an alternative, you can buy prescription safety glasses with shatterproof plastic lenses and built-in side shields. Always wear your safety glasses.

Earmuffs protect your hearing

Router motors make a loud, high-pitched whine. Spend more than a few minutes a day with this noise reverberating in your ears and you will do permanent damage to your hearing ability. The solution is to wear noise-reducing earmuffs or ear plugs. You can buy comfortable muffs with gel-filled cushions. Or you can buy disposable foam plugs that fill the ear canal.

Don't breathe the dust

There are three ways of dealing with dust and chips. You can vacuum them up at the source, or you can filter them out of the air you breathe, or do both. Which method you choose depends on your equipment as well as on your own sensitivity — some people develop terrible wood-dust allergies and can't stand to breathe any of it, and dust-induced nasal cancer is an occupational hazard of full-time woodworkers.

It's easy to connect a shop vacuum to a router table. Most commercial fences include a dust-collection port. Some newer routers have ingenious fittings for sucking the dust and chips away from the router cutter itself.

Dust masks are only marginally effective against the amount of air-borne crud a router can kick up, and they're worthless over beards. You can find fresh-air mask systems that blow fresh air through a plastic helmet and face shield, effectively keeping all dust away from your mouth and nose. If wood dust is a problem for you, this is the way to go.

Setting up your new router

You've weighed the alternatives and chosen the perfect router. You're ready to take it out of the box and put it to work. It will pay to spend a few minutes going over the machine first. Follow these steps:

Read the owner's manual and safety instructions.

Clean shipping grease off smooth metal parts.

Remove the collet and any accessory fittings.

Remove the router motor from the base and reinstall it.

Run the depth mechanism to its limits, then lock it at an intermediate setting.

Go over all the metal castings. Look for burrs, metal flashing, and any other stray crud. Remove it with a small, fine file.

Go over all moveable fittings. Make sure set screws, gears, pinions, and threads are clean and correctly assembled, not cross-threaded or misaligned. Be sure you understand what each fitting does and how it works.

Plug in the router and start it without the collet. It should run smoothly, with no vibration. Any vibration is a problem you probably cannot fix — return the router to your dealer.

Install the collet and a cutter, tighten the collet securely (page 46), set the depth of cut, and make a test cut in wood.

Remove any burrs and casting marks from the router's base plate with fine sandpaper.

Set up the router for the first time and let the chips fly.

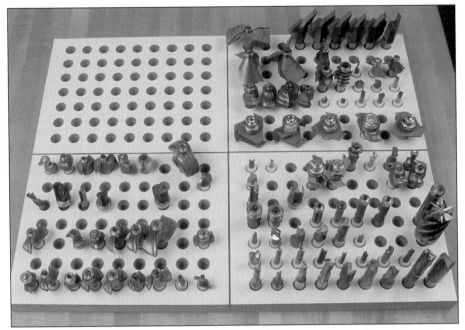

Sea of bits. Your investment in bits can mount up. Store them so they don't damage one another by banging around loosely, and so you can find the one you're looking for. These aftermarket trays each have 63 holes and come with plastic inserts for 1/4-inch (6mm) bits.

Chapter Three

Router Bits

In the old days, a cabinetmaker would own dozens of different molding planes and perhaps a universal plane with many interchangeable cutters. Routers have replaced specialized planes, and today's marketplace sports hundreds of different router bits.

The good news is that you don't have to buy all the different kinds of bits. You can start with a few careful selections. Then you can add to your collection as the need arises. Once you have a basic collection of bits, you'll be able to solve most routing problems and complete most operations without another trip down that profit-spinning aisle.

There are so many router bits that it's essential to sort them into categories, even though few categories can be air-tight or exclusive. I'll discuss several ways of creating order in what appears to be router-bit chaos.

Manufacturers' claims

Manufacturers of router bits are constantly changing their products, and in general the changes are improvements. Most manufacturers are quick to use new materials and coatings that cut better, hold a sharper edge, and stay sharp longer. They are also quick to introduce new profiles and new cutter geometries. This puts the woodworker in the spot of being hit with claims of all sorts for products within a wide price range. Some claims can be verified by looking closely at the bit. Some claims you can't verify for yourself, for example:

The quality of the steel, tungsten carbide, or other materials.

Machining tolerances in forming the bit.

Concentricity of cutting edges and shaft.

My solution is to rely on two guides: price, and the brand name or reputation of the manufacturer. As with most tooling, you generally get what you pay for. Since the same manufacturers supply cutters to the woodworking industry as to amateur woodworkers, hucksters with deflated prices don't survive for long.

Trust your eyes and fingertips

Whenever you buy a router bit, whatever kind of bit it is, take a good, close look at it. Check that the cutting edges are sound and clean, with no nicks or chips. If you can open the package, feel for nicks by running your thumbnail along the cutting edge. Look at the metal and at the weld between the bit body and the carbide insert. There should be no sign of pitting or pinholes.

At the end of the day your own experience using the bit is what matters. Cut some wood and check the cut.

Guiding the bit

From a working point of view, there are three different kinds of router bits:

Bits without pilots,

Bits with tip-mounted pilots,

Bits with shank-mounted pilots.

Bits without pilots require an external guide, such as a fence or a guide collar. They can pierce the surface of the workpiece, so they can be used to form slots, grooves, and recesses. They can also be used to shape all or part of an edge.

Bits with pilots at the tip can be guided by the unshaped portion of the workpiece edge, or they can follow a template. Edge-guided piloted bits can shape part of an edge (a portion must remain uncut to guide the bit). Template-guided bits with pilots can shape all of an edge — they're guided by the template, not by the existing workpiece edge. However, bits with pilots at the tip cannot pierce the surface of the workpiece to form a groove or an excavation someplace in the middle.

Bits without pilots

Shank-mounted pilots

Bits with tip-mounted pilots

Interchangeable pilot bearings

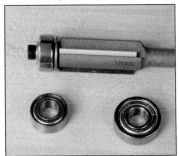

Bits with pilots at the shank must be guided by a template fastened onto the workpiece. They can shape all or part of the workpiece edge. They also can pierce the surface of the workpiece to form a groove or recess away from an edge, provided you arrange some other way to guide the cut, as you would for a bit with no pilot. In this situation the shank-mounted ball-bearing is not actually involved.

Whether or not there is a pilot on the bit determines how it can be used, but it doesn't follow that you should prefer one variety over the other. Before long you will need bits of all three types.

It's best to avoid bits with solid-steel pilots, because they spin at the same speed as the router motor, generating heat from friction and compressing the wood. The heat is likely to scorch the workpiece, and scorch marks are extremely difficult to sand out.

Free-spinning ball-bearing pilots don't burn the workpiece. If the bearing freezes, it's usually replaceable by removing the center screw.

Bits with solid-steel pilots

Vertical and horizontal panel-raising bits

Slot-cutter with interchangeable blades

Cope-and-stick bit set

Shank diameter

Bits often are sold and cataloged by shank diameter. In the US market, there are only two possibilities.

1/4 inch,

1/2 inch.

In the European market, bits are sized and sold in metric sizes, typically:

6mm,

12mm.

You're always better off with the largest bit shank your router will accept. You'll have a cleaner cut with less vibration and less stress on the machine. Small bits aren't always available with a 1/2-inch (12mm) shank, but all 1/2-inch (12mm) routers will accept a 1/4-inch (6mm) collet or collet adapter.

Bits with a 1/4-inch (6mm) shank and a cutting diameter of 1-1/2 inch (36mm) or more are dangerous and should be avoided. They've been marketed to increase the potential of small routers, even though those routers lack the power to make anything but the smallest cut. If you mount large, 1/4-inch (6mm) shank bits in a router that does have enough power, the shank itself is at risk of bending or snapping off.

European metric sizes are not an exact match with US sizes. A 12mm shank will not fit a 1/2-inch collet, nor vice-versa. The 3/8-inch shank, and the European equivalent, 8mm, are rapidly disappearing from the marketplace.

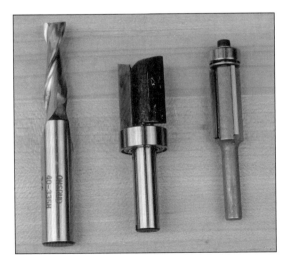

Bits with 1/2-inch, 3/8-inch, and 1/4-inch shanks

The 1/4-inch shank isn't enough for this large bit.

Bit material

There are three ways to make router bits. They can be:

Cast and machined from high-speed steel,

Cast steel body with tungsten-carbide tips welded on,

Machined from solid tungsten carbide with a steel shank.

High-speed steel

Carbide-tipped

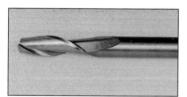

Solid carbide

Steel making and steel forming techniques are the stuff of constant research by companies large and small throughout the world. They are always searching for better results at lower cost. We are the recipients of this technology and it shows in the router bits available to us.

The advantage of carbide is that it stays sharp a lot longer than high-speed steel. It's difficult to say how much longer, but anywhere from four to eight times is typical, depending on the material being cut.

Although modern carbide is much less prone to chipping than it was in former days, carbide will chip. To avoid chipping, keep the router bit from contacting other metals, and always enter the cut gently, especially in hardwoods.

While most manufacturers will give you some information about the composition of their steel and carbide, the only thing you can rely on is that high-speed steel is cheaper than carbide-tipped, which is cheaper than solid carbide. You will find almost every bit type made in each material.

Edge profile

The cutting edge itself is the sharp part. The flute is the cavity ahead of the edge, where the chips accumulate. All the rest of the routing apparatus exists solely to steer the whirling edges into the workpiece. The profile of the cutting edge is the cross-section it will cut into the workpiece. Although you will find an enormous number of router bit profiles, they can be sorted into four categories:

Straight and parallel,

Straight and not parallel,

Curved,

Complex.

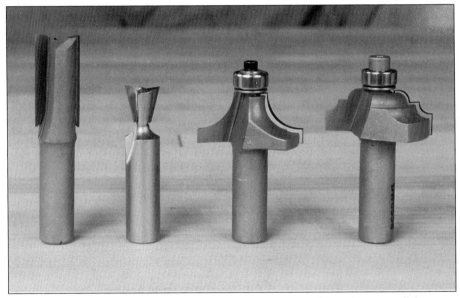

Edge profiles: straight and parallel, straight and not parallel, curved, and complex.

Edge geometry

The geometry of the bit describes the relationship of the cutting edges relative to the axis of rotation. Edge geometry has many aspects, four of which will be considered here:

Number of edges,

Cutting angle,

Flute depth,

Hook angle and cutter clearance.

The smoothness of the cut results largely from the relationship between these four factors. For the most part, edge geometry does not depend on the cutting profile. These same factors apply whether the bit is straight, curved, or complex. And while you can't change a bit's edge geometry, understanding it will help you choose the bit that will give the best performance for your money.

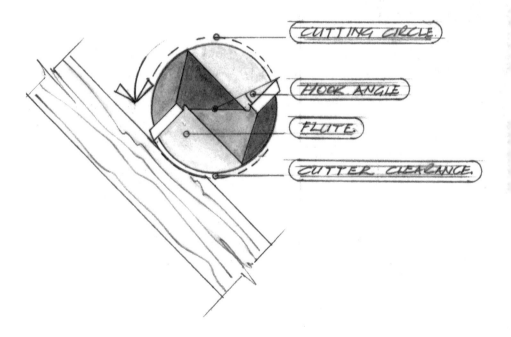

End view of a bit with two cutting edges

Number of cutting edges

The least number of cutting edges is one. For general stock removal at the lowest price, a single-edge bit is the choice. They're normally available in high-speed steel as well as carbide-tipped. However, in diameters larger than about 1/2 inch (12mm), a single-edge bit is liable to be imbalanced and prone to vibration. That's why most bits have two edges. They're more expensive than single edges to manufacture, but they are the easiest to balance. While you sometimes find three-edge bits, and they do a fine job, they're rare and expensive.

Two edges and six edges

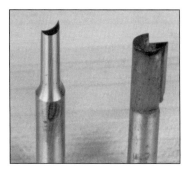

Single edge

Cutting angle

The cutting angle is the slope of the edges with respect to the vertical axis of the shank. Cutting angle is the most important factor in determining how smoothly the bit will work. There are three possibilities:

The edges can be **parallel** to the axis,

The edges can be skewed at a **small angle** to the axis,

The edges can form a **spiral**, or more correctly, a helix.

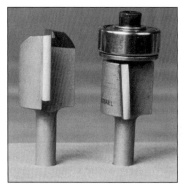

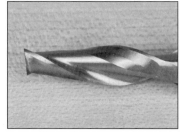

Spiral edges

Straight edge and skewed edge

A **parallel edge**, which is the most common design, bangs into the work each time it goes around. For most of each revolution, the edge fans the air. This cutting action is very much like that of a jointer or thickness planer. Because it contacts the work intermittently, parallel edges leave a series of milling marks on the wood, the same as a jointer does. The spacing of these mill marks depends upon the feed speed. A slow speed produces fine, closely spaced, and all but invisible marks, while a rapid feed leaves wide ripples that will be very difficult to sand away.

A **skewed edge** shears the wood off the workpiece. It makes shavings, not chips. Although the edge spends more of each revolution in the workpiece, it still hits intermittently. Compared to parallel edges, skewed-edge bits are less likely to vibrate and more likely to leave a smooth surface with no visible mill marks.

Six edges

Spiral edges not only shear the wood, they also cut continuously. Some part of the edge is always in the workpiece, so there's no vibration from the impact of entering and leaving the wood. Consequently they produce shavings, and leave a smooth surface with no mill marks. They're also quiet, which makes for a different routing experience.

Spiral bits can be made of high-speed steel, special steels, or solid carbide, with a single edge or with multiple edges, or "starts." Large bits may have up to six starts.

Up-cutting spiral, right, and down-cutting spiral

Spiral flutes have a direction. The helix can twist upward as the bit rotates, or it can twist downward. Both designs cut equally well, but the chips tend to fly in the direction of the spiral. Thus an up-cutting spiral lifts the chips out of the workpiece toward the router, while a down-cutting spiral tends to throw them downward, away from the router. One variety is not any better than the other, it all depends on the cutting situation.

Because spiral bits don't vibrate and do leave a smooth surface, they're ideal for cutting mortises and slots. In fact spiral bits have made it possible to develop a new and effective kind of joint, the loose tenon (page 143).

Spiral bits are not yet common, but they are such a significant improvement that they are becoming more widely available all the time. Bits with spiral edges are expensive to manufacture, but the technology is not new — it's standard practice in metalworking.

Flute depth

A problem in router-bit design is clearing the chips. Chips expand to about three times the volume of the original wood. When chips pack up around the bit, cutting efficiency decreases, frictional heat increases, and a scorched workpiece is the likely result.

When router bits get larger than 5/8 inch in diameter, better manufacturers apply an engineering standard that keeps the cutting edge from extending more than about .05 inch beyond the bit body. This controls the size of the chip that can be removed on each revolution. Similarly, on most large bits the bit body itself is essentially circular in cross-section. This helps balance the bit and also helps limit the chip size.

Sharpening router bits

High-speed steel bits can be sharpened — once — on a fine waterstone, and with small slipstones lubricated with water. Sharpen carefully, maintaining the original bevel angles. On two-flute bits, try to do the same amount of work on each flute. At 22,000 RPM, a small difference in weight can generate a dangerous vibration.

Although people will try to touch up carbide bits with a diamond hone, it's difficult to get a good result. Some manufacturers will resharpen carbide bits of simple profile. Complex profiles can't be sharpened because removing material changes the shape. When you've got a blunt carbide bit, my advice is to toss it and buy another.

Sharpen steel bits with slips and on the edge of a fine stone. Sharpen the flat side, leaving the shaped part of the edge alone.

Cleaning bits and collets

It's good practice to strip the router after each working session, not to leave it set up until the next time you need it. Clean router bits and collets as you remove them and return them to storage. If you delay, the moisture and chemicals in the wood dust will act on the metal, rust will begin to form, and the parts are likely to lock together.

Cleaning amounts to wiping with a clean, slightly oily rag. The oil prevents rust, so the humidity in your shop will dictate how much oil goes on the rag. Bit shanks should not be allowed to collect surface rust, but they shouldn't feel oily either.

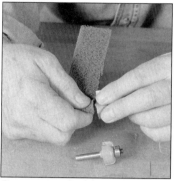

Remove crud with Scoth-Brite.

Stubborn crud and light rust can be removed with a fine Scotch-Brite pad, or with a round, brass-bristle brush of the type used to clean guns. A bit with a lot of pitch on it can be left overnight in a jar of alcohol, then cleaned with Scotch-Brite.

Inspect the shank of the cutter as you clean it. The metal should be smooth. Score marks or gray deposits (called galls) indicate slipping in the collet. Either the collet was not tightened, or the collet is worn out, and you may have to replace both bit and collet.

Clean collets with a brass brush.

Clean collets with a fine, brass-bristle brush of the type used to maintain firearms, and keep them lightly oiled as well.

You'll work out your own storage system, but shank-sized holes drilled in a block of wood are hard to beat. Drill the storage holes 1/64 inch (.5mm) larger than the bit shank.

Even here, the aftermarket manufacturers have come to the rescue. You can buy plastic trays with holes for bits, and some even have flip-down lids. While I haven't seen any real improvement on the drilled block of wood, it is important to take the storage problem seriously and to organize a solution that suits you. Modern bits and collets are far too delicate and expensive to leave banging around loose in a box.

Store bits so they can't bang together.

Locking the bit in the collet

When you tighten the lock nut with a wrench, it pushes the collet into the tapered hole, which squeezes the slits together so they grip the bit shank. Some routers require a second wrench to keep the motor shaft from turning. Others have a spring-loaded bar that clicks into a hole in the motor shaft to lock it. The pitch of the lock nut thread is small, so bearing down on the wrench causes the collet to hold the bit very tightly and no amount of vibration will work it loose.

Once the lock nut comes to a stop, give the wrench a small nip and that's tight enough. If you find you have to strain to loosen the lock nut, you over-tightened it in the first place.

Older, single-slit collets often have trouble releasing the bit. The lock nut compresses the tapers together so efficiently that you have to persuade it with a soft mallet or a sharp rap on the bit shank. Poor maintenance makes the situation worse, by adding the glue power of crud and rust.

The lock nut draws the collet against the taper in the motor shaft. This squeezes the slotted collet tight around the bit shank.

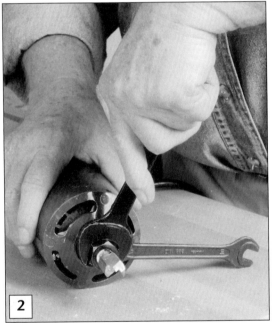

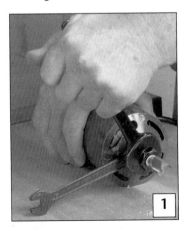

Fixed-base routers require two wrenches, one on the collet nut and the other holding flats on the motor shaft. To change bits, always remove the motor from the router base. Brace the motor wrench on the bench while you tighten (1) or loosen (2) the collet itself.

The new, multi-slit collets get over the problem. Manufacturers' solutions differ in detail, but the heart of all of them is a groove in the lock nut, which fits a tiny bead on the collet rim. When you turn the lock nut to remove the bit, it loosens for one turn, then it tightens again before spinning free. This is the lock nut pulling the tapered collet out of the shaft so it can open to release the bit shank.

Keep the bit *shoulder clear of the collet.*

Newer routers also have a longer collet than old ones, so the full shank of the bit can slide home without bottoming out. When you insert the bit, don't push it so deep that the collet rides onto the radiused shoulder between cutter and shank, and don't let it bottom out. Keep about 1/8 inch of shank visible outside the collet. If the collet catches the shoulder, it won't tighten securely. If the bit bottoms out, the collet action is likely to score the shank, perhaps damaging the mechanism as well.

The day will come when you want to rout deep and the only way is to project more bit out of the collet. The situation is dangerous, and the bigger the cutting circle, the greater the risk. You can minimize risk by keeping at least 1/2 inch (12mm) of the shank in the collet, and by taking a small cut.

Some low-price routers have two-piece or two-slot collets. You can also find collet adapters, which are metal sleeves for fitting 1/4-inch (6mm) shanks into a 1/2-inch (12mm) collet.

It's important to keep the collet absolutely clean and lubricated with a very thin film of oil. Clean both the tapered socket in the motor shaft and the shank of the bit. If your workshop tends to be damp, a wipe with an oily rag will help keep these parts free of any trace of surface rust.

Plunge routers vary. Some have a button or lever to lock the motor shaft. They require only one wrench. Others require two wrenches, same as a fixed-base machine.

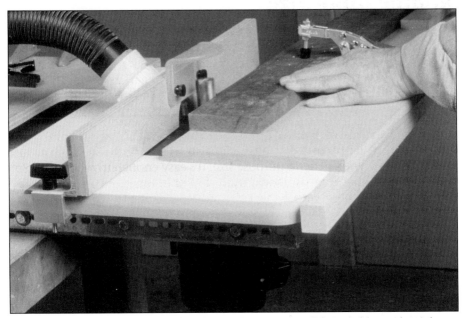

Bench-hung router table is stable, at the right height, and doesn't use much shop space.

Chapter Four

Router Table

The router table expands the already vast capabilities of the router. Essentially it is a work surface with the router mounted underneath it, so the bit sticks up through the top. The table fixes the router in one position, while the operator feeds the workpiece into the cutter. Every router-table operation requires some method of guiding the workpiece. The three choices are a **straight fence**, a **split fence**, or a **pilot bearing** on the router bit (see page 82).

Router tables are extremely useful, and they're straightforward to set up and use. Consequently, making router tables has been a prime focus of magazine articles and book chapters. It's easy to find plans for free-standing units with built-in storage cabinets, for bench-top units, and for everything in between. One good result of all this activity has been the welcome appearance of products designed to help woodworkers construct good router tables, including tops, fences, base plates, guards, and dust hoods.

In this chapter I'll share the design of a router table I use and like, which has not appeared elsewhere. I'll describe it in terms of the issues that every table design must address.

Router table size

The router table should be the size that suits your own work the best. Though most tables are wider than they are deep, there are no absolute rules. Usually the router is centered. The table top needs room at the front and sides for the workpiece plus any work-holding jig, with room at the back for the fence and dust-collection apparatus, and an opening for clamps.

I've found 18 inches (45cm) by 24 inches (60cm) to be a good general-purpose size. It's easy enough to mock up a plywood or cardboard table top, and see how it handles your typical workpieces.

The thing to avoid is a table with a tiny top. The router cutout is liable to leave too little margin for stability, and it will limit the size of work you can safely manage.

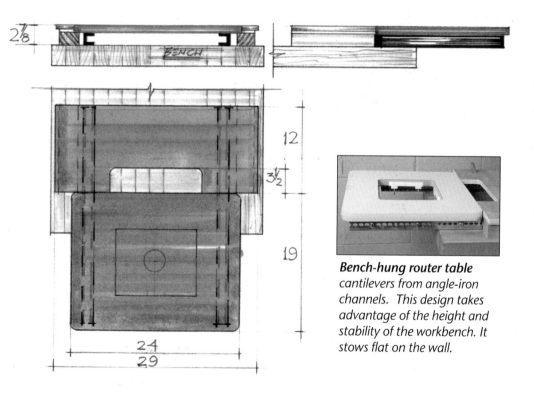

Bench-hung router table cantilevers from angle-iron channels. This design takes advantage of the height and stability of the workbench. It stows flat on the wall.

Supporting the router table

The table has to be stable, sturdy, and at a comfortable working height. While many woodworkers prefer to make a cabinet-style base, others have a shop that is just too small. My solution is to use the workbench as the platform. It's already the most sturdy and stable platform I can devise. The table top mounts on two substantial rails, which cantilever from the bench and secure with a couple of clamps. This setup automatically puts the table top at a comfortable working height, it guarantees stability, and it doesn't eat up any floor space. When it's not in use, the router table hangs on the wall, out of the way.

If you design your own table base, make sure it is big enough to be stable and is at the height that's right for you. Most machine tables are 36 inches (90cm) high, which suits people of average physique. Six inches (15cm) higher isn't a problem, though I wouldn't go any lower.

Height is the big problem with a table that perches on top of the workbench. Enough height to accommodate a mid-size router puts the working surface somewhere near your chin, too high for comfort and safety.

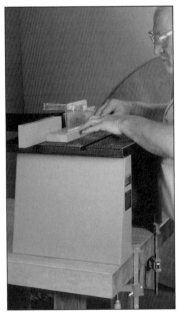

Clamped to the bench, this aftermarket table is too high. It needs its own low stand.

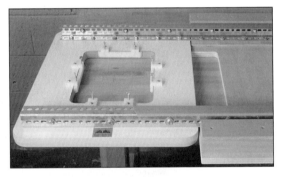

Bench-hung router table from below: Bolt the support rails together from lengths of angle iron.

Top material

The table top has to be smooth, stiff, and sturdy. Plastic laminate on 1-inch (25mm) MDF is an excellent solution. While you could make up such a top for yourself, you'll find a range of sizes at attractive prices in woodworking catalogs that specialize in router gear. In fact, you'll find it is cheaper to buy the top ready-made than to make it for yourself.

Mounting the router

The router has to be mounted upside-down on a plate that fits flush with the surface of the top. To change bits and adjust the depth of cut, the plate and router have to be easy to remove. The plate has to be rigid, yet thin enough to not crowd the router bit. The mounting mechanism has to be secure, yet adjustable to level the insert with the table surface. This is another area where router entrepreneurs can offer finished parts for less money than it would cost you to buy the materials.

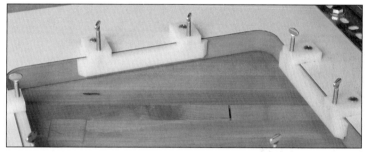

Table top from below: Thumbscrews move plastic mounting rails, which adjust the height of the large base plate.

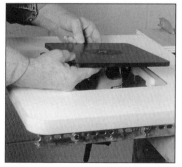

Screw the router to the large base plate, and drop it into the table opening.

Adjust the thumbscrews to level the base plate with the table surface.

Fences for the router table

Three kinds of fence can be used on the router table:

Straight or **continuous,**

Split,

Pilot bearing on bit.

The **straight** or **continuous fence,** like a table-saw fence, goes across the table top. It's for shaping part of the edge of the workpiece, where the uncut portion of the edge guides the cut. In all setups, part of the bit is housed inside the fence. The cutout for the bit can also act as a dust-collection port. When you want to stand the workpiece up on edge, you'll need a high version of the regular straight fence.

The **split** or **two-part fence** divides on the infeed and outfeed sides of the bit. Both parts have to move and be independently clamped. This arrangement allows you to rout the entire edge of the workpiece. The infeed fence starts the operation. Then the newly cut surface, bearing on the outfeed fence, guides it to completion. Photos on page 54 show exactly how to set the split fence.

You can buy both kinds of fence from the mail-order catalogs. You can also make them from plywood or MDF, so long as you ensure that they are rigid, adjustable, and clampable. The drawing on the facing page shows one good design. The little rebate on the bottom edge of the fence prevents stray chips from interfering with the workpiece.

The third kind of fence, **pilot bearing on bit**, guides the cut by running along part of the workpiece edge or along a template attached to the workpiece. The setup requires a starting pin. Otherwise, the workpiece would get involved with the cutter before it could reach the stability of the bearing. It could be pulled out of your hands, or spoiled, or both.

The starting pin is a post plugged into the router plate about 2 inches (5cm) from the cutter. It's a piece of wood or hard plastic rod about 1/2 inch (12mm) in diameter by 1-1/4 (3cm) inches long. To start the cut, brace the edge of the workpiece against the pin, then pivot it firmly into the cutter. Once the workpiece edge or template contacts the pilot bearing, pivot the workpiece off the starting pin. The bearing guides the rest of the cut, the pin has no further role.

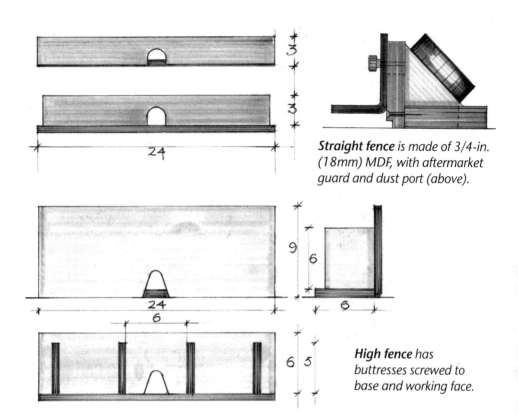

Straight fence is made of 3/4-in. (18mm) MDF, with aftermarket guard and dust port (above).

High fence has buttresses screwed to base and working face.

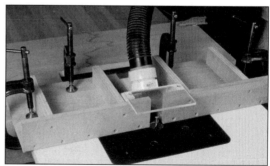

The split fence allows you to shape the entire edge of the workpiece. The two parts move independently, to compensate for the depth of cut. Make the parts about 12 inches (30 cm) long.

The straight fence is the most convenient setup for making rebates and molding edges. To stand the workpiece up on end, make a high version of the fence. All these fences clamp directly to the router table.

Setting the split fence

The two parts of the split fence adjust independently. This permits the workpiece to remain in solid contact with the fence throughout the cut. To set the fence, follow these steps.

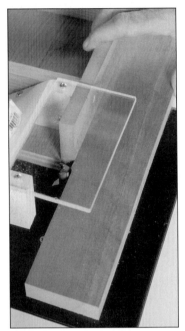

1. Set the infeed fence to the depth of cut and start the cut. Stop the router.

2. Hold or clamp the workpiece *against the infeed fence, and bring the outfeed fence into contact with the newly cut edge.*

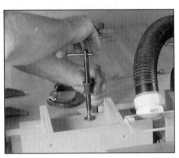

3. Clamp the outfeed fence to the router table.

4. Restart the router and feed the workpiece onto the outfeed fence.

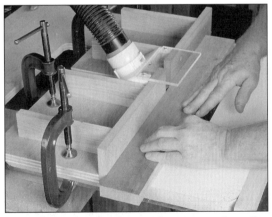

5. As the cut proceeds, *transfer pressure from the infeed fence to the outfeed fence.*

Miter sled

Many router tables have a 3/4 inch (18mm) by 3/8 inch (9mm) groove across the top, which accepts a standard miter gauge. The miter gauge will support and stabilize the workpiece, and it also helps you make joints by routing across the end of the wood. If your table doesn't have a slot, you can rout one. As an alternative, you can use the front edge of the table to guide a sled, as shown in the photo below.

Front rail guides Masonite miter sled. To rout across the end of a workpiece, clamp it to the right-angle fence.

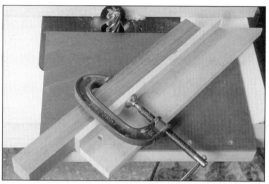

To miter the workpiece, and to rout across a mitered end, screw a 45-degree fence to the sled. Clamp the workpiece to the fence. For details on making sleds like these, see page 124.

Dust and chip exhaust

The router is exceedingly messy. It makes millions of tiny little chips, plus a lot of dust. Fifteen minutes of serious routing without a dust exhaust could leave you with an hour of clean-up. Fortunately, the manufacturers and after-market entrepreneurs have come to the rescue, with ready-made dust fittings that hook up to a standard shop vacuum.

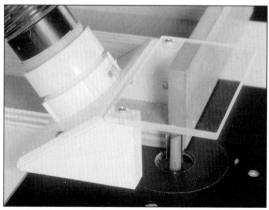

Dust port, safety guard screwed to infeed fence

Safety guard

For a useful reminder of where not to put your fingers, screw a plastic top guard to the router table fence. On a split fence, screw the guard to the dust port, then screw the dust port to the infeed fence.

Measuring tools are the keys to accuracy.

Chapter Five

The Keys to Accuracy

Accuracy is a relative term. It depends on the material, on your measuring tools, and on your objective. Accuracy in soft materials like leather is not the same as accuracy in wood, and accuracy in hard materials like metal is different again. Woodworkers are concerned with three different kinds of accuracy:

Dimensional accuracy,

Angular accuracy,

Surface regularity.

When you are routing wood, accuracy depends on a chain of events primarily involving the setup and guide system. Depending on what you are making, acceptable accuracy in wood varies across three full orders of magnitude, from +/-1 inch to .001 inch (25 mm to .025 mm).

Dimensional accuracy varies by about one order of magnitude, from 1/8 inch or 1/10 inch (2mm to 3mm) to 1/64 inch (.5mm) or 1/100 inch (.25mm). If you are building a house, cutting a 2x4 to within 1/8 inch (3mm) of the mark is close enough. If you are making a fine piece of furniture, +/- 1/8 inch (3mm) is far too crude, but a tolerance of +/- .01 inch (.25mm) is close enough. More to the point, that's about the limit of accuracy you can achieve with ordinary woodworking tools in a material as variable as wood. In most woodworking, making parts that are all the same size, or that will fit a given space the way a drawer front fits its opening, is more important than precisely specified dimensions.

Angular accuracy normally is not a matter of plus or minus. Something is either square or it isn't. However, if you were to measure angular accuracy with sophisticated instruments, you would find that normal woodworking accuracy is within a minute of arc, that is, 1/60 of a degree.

Surface regularity has three aspects:

Flatness,

Twist,

Smoothness.

The first two can be checked with a straight edge and winding sticks. These tools will reveal deviations from flat of about .01 inch (.25mm). However, a smoothing plane or a finely set shear-cutting router bit can take a shaving that is .001 inch (.025mm) in thickness, and your fingertips can detect the difference.

It is difficult to measure surface smoothness, though it is easy to assess it by touch.

Measure the wood, not the router

To check the router's performance, observe and measure the wood. Of course you begin by setting up the router with your measuring tools and in most cases the results will be a true reflection of the setup. However, on occasion it won't be what you expect. The setup is only as accurate as the results, and an accurately routed workpiece is what matters.

Measuring and marking tools

No matter what router you own, if you are striving for accuracy you need measuring and marking tools. You must have all of these tools in order to set up your router and check the accuracy of the workpiece — there are no shortcuts. These tools are not specific to the router. You can use them to assess the condition of any machine, and the results of any woodworking operation, whether done by hand or machine.

The kit of measuring tools used in this book includes:

Straight edge, 24 inch (60 cm). Assesses flatness.

Pair of **winding sticks**, 20 inch (50cm). Measures twist.

Squares with graduated rule. Verifies 90 degrees.

Dial caliper. Measures small distances.

Metal **tape measure**, 1 inch x 25 feet (25mm x 6m). Measures large distances.

Protractor and **sliding bevel**. Measures angles.

Hand lens, 4x magnification. Helps you see.

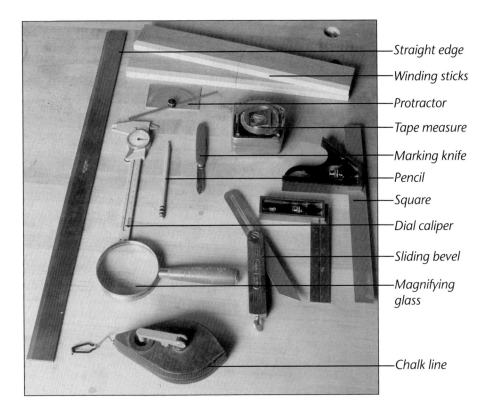

Straight edge
Winding sticks
Protractor
Tape measure
Marking knife
Pencil
Square
Dial caliper
Sliding bevel
Magnifying glass
Chalk line

Checking dimensional accuracy

Dimensional accuracy means you want to be able to rout pieces of wood that are the same size over and over again. It's rarely a matter of a single piece of wood, it's dimensioning a number of pieces identically. While the right size can be a specific measurement, woodworkers more often work to a fit: The drawer fits the opening, the joint shoulders are the same distance apart.

There are two ways to check dimensional accuracy.

Measure the wood,

Directly observe the wood.

To measure the wood, use a ruler, tape measure, or dial caliper. Your choice of instrument depends on the span in question. With a ruler, use a stop block to establish the zero point — your fingertip is too uncertain.

For direct observation, the tools are your eyes and fingertips. Rout two pieces of wood using the same setup and fit them together. Orient both face sides the same way, one piece on top of the other. You will be able to see, and feel, whether or not they are the same size. Your fingertips can detect size differences of less than .001 inch (.025mm).

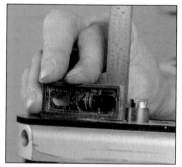

Set up the router by measuring it, but check the results by measuring the wood.

The fingertips give direct feedback as to whether the joint is flush or not. Any discrepancy is difficult to measure but easy to feel.

Dial caliper

A dial caliper measures distances to a high degree of accuracy. It can make inside measurements as well as outside ones, so it can measure the thickness of the workpiece, the width of a groove, and the depth of a groove.

While you could spend a lot of money for a machinist's caliper with a digital readout, there are two affordable alternatives. Most hardware stores sell a sturdy plastic caliper with a green dial. It measures 64ths and 100ths of an inch. As an alternative, most metalworking suppliers sell imported, low-priced dial calipers that measure to .001 inch (.025mm).

To use a caliper, plant the fixed jaw on the workpiece and press it there with your finger. Then bring the movable jaw into contact with the wood. Be sure the caliper sits squarely on the wood and isn't cocked to either side.

If you don't have a dial caliper, get one. You will wonder how you ever got along without it.

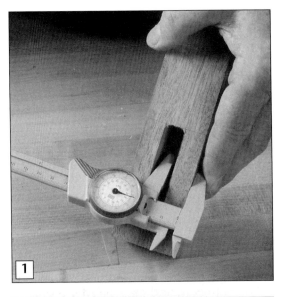

Using the dial caliper: Plant the fixed jaw squarely on the workpiece (1), then bring the movable jaw into contact (2).

Tape measure

A 25-foot (8m or 10m) steel tape is always close to hand for most woodworkers. Although it can measure all distances up to the length of the tape, the steel rule and dial caliper are more accurate over small distances.

If you check one tape against another, you'll be surprised by how much they vary. It usually doesn't matter, as long as you use the same tape throughout a job.

One subtlety of the steel tape is the hook that keeps it from retracting into its case. The hook is always loose on its rivets, and it's supposed to be that way. The amount of looseness corresponds to the thickness of the hook itself, which makes the tape accurate for inside measure as well as for outside measure.

Checking angular accuracy

Angular accuracy, most of the time, means square, 90 degrees, precisely. It's either square or it isn't.

Use the square to check the newly routed edge in two places, a couple of inches in from either end of the board. There are only three possible conditions:

It's square at both ends. You can assume it's also square all along the length.

It's not square, but the deviation is about the same at either end. Check the setup, correct it, and rout the edge again.

It's not square, but the deviation shifts from one side of the wood to the other — the routed edge twists. The most likely cause is that the face of the wood is not flat, so check it with your winding sticks.

Caring for squares

Dropping and banging around may raise a burr on one corner of the square. You'll feel it as you lower the stock onto the workpiece. Remove the burr on 400-grit carborundum paper held flat on a sheet of glass.

Square

You can buy a fixed-blade square or a combination square, which has a moveable, graduated blade. The blade can be removed and used as a rule for measuring distances up to its own length, which can be 4, 6, 12, 18 or 24 inches, or their metric equivalents.

Quality makes a real difference. Buy an accurately made machinist's square, not a crude imitation. Good brands are Starrett in the US, and Moore & Wright in the UK. One way to tell the difference at a glance is by looking at the graduations incised into the metal rule, or blade. They should be fine and precise, not crude, paint-filled stampings.

To use the combination square to assess a piece of wood, slide the stock toward the center of the rule and tighten the thumbscrew. Place the stock firmly against the face or edge of the wood, then lower it until the rule makes contact. Don't slide it like a trombone, because the square has to be stationary to give you an accurate reading.

When you hold the wood against the square, you're looking for any deviation. Unlike our tools for measuring dimensions, which tell you exactly how big the wood is, the square doesn't produce an angular measurement other than 90 degrees. It's either square or it isn't. The same is true at 45 degrees, which combination squares can also verify.

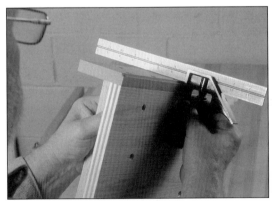

Press the stock of the square against the wood, then lower the blade onto it. Look toward the light and you will see any deviation from 90 degrees.

Sliding bevel and protractor

The sliding bevel is the traditional tool for managing angles other than 90 degrees. While it does not measure an angle, it allows you to transfer one from drawing to workpiece or from one workpiece to another.

In order to measure angles, you have to borrow a tool from the nearest fourth-grade child, the plastic protractor.

It's often difficult to directly measure an angle on the wood itself. Instead, take the angle with the sliding bevel and transfer it to the bench top or to a piece of paper. Then measure the drawing with the protractor.

In most woodworking applications, the precise value of an angle matters less than achieving a consistent angle from one workpiece to the next. When you are making a closed construction, you have to expect to adjust the last piece to bring everything into line.

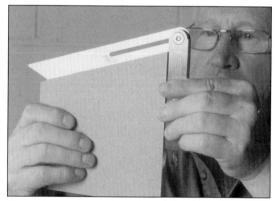

To measure an angle, take it off the wood with the sliding bevel.

Transfer the angle to the edge of a board.

Measure the transferred angle with the machinist's protractor, left, or with a plastic school protractor.

Checking surface regularity

The third aspect of accuracy is surface regularity. You can assess flatness with a straight edge and winding sticks. To assess smoothness, however, the only tools woodworkers have are the eye and hand.

The 4x magnifying glass can tell you how your tools are performing. The marks left by the router bit are an important diagnostic tool. They are the clue to knowing whether you are feeding the wood correctly, whether you have set the fence correctly, and whether the bit is damaged.

Straight edge

A straight edge assesses straightness. It doesn't do anything else. It's not a ruler or a yardstick. It is a precision instrument. A good one is expensive, but it really is essential. The 24-inch (60cm) size is good for general woodworking and machine tune-up. It will be accurate to within .0005 inch.

When you are doing accurate work, the straight edge has to be close at hand. Since its value depends totally on its accurate edge, you must take care to keep from damaging it. When you're using the straight edge to check the flatness of a surface, set it gently on the work. Don't bang it around. Lay it flat on the bench, not balanced on other stuff.

Reserve the beveled side of the straight edge for checking straightness of surfaces. Use its back edge as a guide for trimming leather or veneers. Keep it clean and bright.

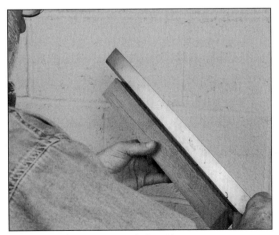

A straight edge assesses straightness.

Winding sticks

Winding sticks measure twist. They come in pairs and they are shop made.

The important requirement of a winding stick is that its long edges be parallel. Make yourself a couple of pairs, one about 14 inches long and one a short 6 inches. There should be a mark at the center of each stick. Shop-made sticks often have the top edge of inlaid ebony or holly, for easy visibility.

Winding sticks are easy to use. Place each stick across the workpiece near the ends, parallel to one another, then sight their top edges. Crouch down to do this, line up the center marks on the two sticks, and keep your head straight. You'll be able to see whether the sticks are parallel, and if not, how much the surface twists.

Check flat from one end to the other, but also check from the middle of the workpiece to either end. It's possible for the ends to be true while something strange occurs in between. Use the sticks the same way on the edge of the workpiece.

To assess twist, set the winding sticks on the face or edge of the wood, align the center marks, and sight from one to the other.

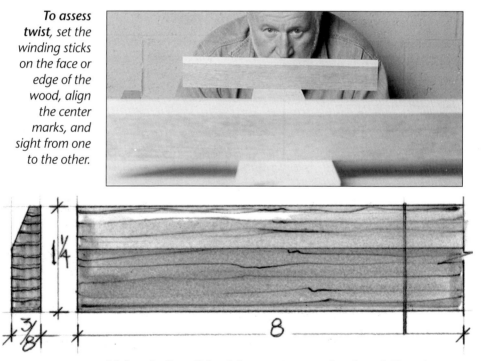

Make winding sticks of dry, quarter-sawn hardwood. The edges must be straight and parallel.

Preparation of stock

Before you can use a router, each piece of wood has to have been made square and to size. The process is called **preparing the stock**. The prepared wood next becomes a **workpiece** to be shaped or changed to suit the needs of the project. Whatever you are going to make, no matter what tools or machines you intend to use, the first thing you have to do is get each piece of wood ready. Since it's vital to the accurate use of a router, here is the preparation sequence, beginning with rough-sawn wood.

1. Prepare a **face side**.

2. Prepare a **face edge**.

3. Saw and plane to width and make the second edge parallel to the face edge.

4. Plane to thickness and make the second face parallel to the face side.

5. Make one end square.

6. Make the second end square and to length.

A **face side** has three characteristics. It is flat in length, flat in width, and doesn't twist. A **face edge** has four characteristics. It is flat in length, flat in width, doesn't twist, and is square to the face side.

To assess the face side and the face edge, you need a straight edge, winding sticks, and a square. How you achieve the face side and edge depends on what equipment you have. It can be done entirely with a hand plane; the machine of choice is a jointer. When you use the jointer, always plane the face side first, mark it with a face side mark, then plane a face edge that is square to the face side and mark that. Face side and face edge marks record the actual condition of the wood. They're not hopeful declarations of intention.

When you work without these reference surfaces, and everyone does so at least part of the time, you can't expect to achieve spot-on accuracy. When you discover that the pieces of wood are not all the same size, or they don't all fit as precisely as you wanted, don't blame the router. Remember that it was you who decided to proceed without creating a face side and face edge. If you want accuracy, you can't skip the process of preparing the stock. It's that simple.

PREPARATION OF STOCK

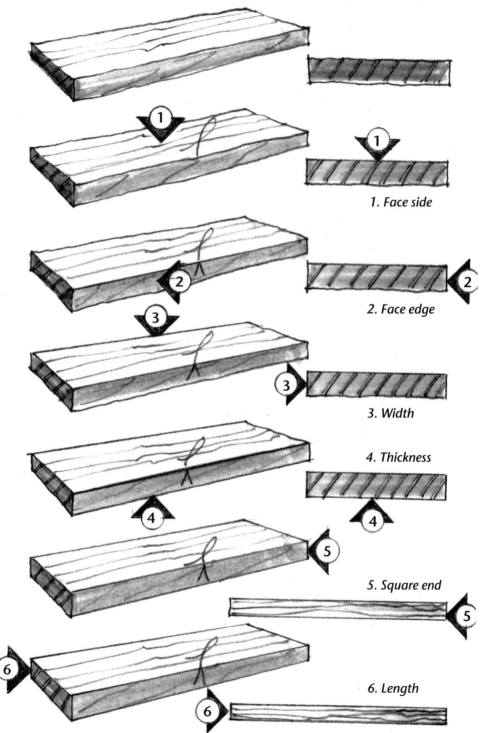

1. Face side

2. Face edge

3. Width

4. Thickness

5. Square end

6. Length

The guide collar follows the template to rout the recess for an inlay.

Chapter Six
Guiding the Router

Considered by itself, the router is an extremely accurate device. Its shaft, collet, and cutter rotate on the motor's axis. Its high speed requires internal bearings that are mechanically excellent. Any deviation would be rotational wobble or runout, in an amount too small to detect without sophisticated instruments.

However, the router motor is only one element in a complex system. The other key elements are:

Router setup,

Guide system,

Workpiece,

Operator.

Each of these elements introduces a set of variables to the routing operation, and each element is another source of inaccuracy. Like a chain that snaps at its weakest link, your entire job can only be as accurate as its most inaccurate aspect. Therefore, in order to achieve accuracy with the router, it's necessary to break the operation down into its parts. That way you can get hold of each variable in turn.

Fence, Guide, Cutting Circle, and Offset

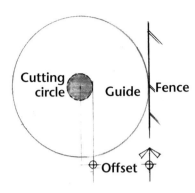

Cutting circle   Guide   Fence

Offset

The guide system is the heart of routing accurately. Each of the seven guide methods turns on the same four elements:

Fence,

Guide,

Cutting circle,

Offset.

The **fence** establishes the path — straight, curved, or complex — that the bit will follow. The fence can be a separate straight edge, it can be the edge of the workpiece itself, or it can be a template. The fence is always separate from the router.

The **guide** is the part of the router that contacts the fence. It can be the edge of the router base plate, a base guide attached to the router base plate, a guide collar, a ball-bearing pilot mounted on the router bit, or a trammel.

The **cutting circle** is the largest diameter of the cut a bit makes.

The **offset** is the distance between the fence and the router bit's cutting circle.

Setup and guide method

The **guide method** is not the same as the **setup.** It is at the heart of it, but the setup also includes clamps, jigs, support blocks, stops, and every other thing you have to do in order to put the guide method into practice.

Measure the offset with a combination square. Press the stock of the square against the guide surface, and rotate the bit to top dead center.

Two basic setups

There are two basic routing setups:

Operator drives router over stationary workpiece,

Operator drives workpiece over table-mounted router.

Operator drives router

When the operator drives the router, the workpiece has to be securely clamped in place. There are four guide systems:

1. Fence attached to workpiece.

2. Guide attached to router base.

3. Pilot on router bit.

4. Guide collar on router base.

Operator drives workpiece

When the operator drives the workpiece, the router has to be securely mounted under a sturdy table, with the bit poking through the top. There are three guide systems for router tables:

5. One-part fence on router table.

6. Two-part fence on router table.

7. Pilot on router bit on router table.

Risk and certainty

If you were guiding the router freehand, the success of the operation would depend entirely on your ability to steer it only where you wanted to cut wood. Throughout the operation, one wrong move would spoil the job. In terminology developed by Prof. David Pye, this is **workmanship of risk**. As you take control of the variable with fences, guides, stop blocks, and hold-downs, you reduce the risk of spoiling the job. Finally, when every aspect of it is under control, you've moved from workmanship of risk to **workmanship of certainty**. When your objective is accuracy, you must reduce the risks by building up the certainties. This requires that you analyze all the variables, and take control of each of them in turn.

Seven guide systems

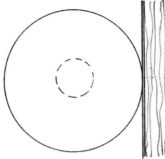

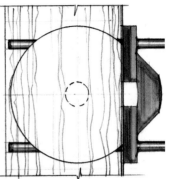

1. Fence attached to workpiece

2. Guide attached to router base

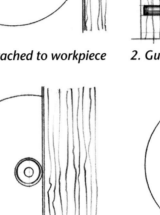

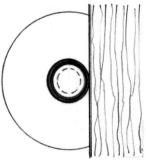

3. Pilot on router bit

4. Guide collar on router base

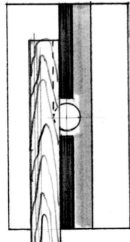

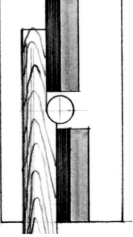

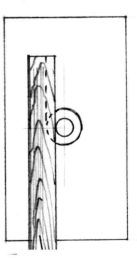

5. One-part fence on
router table

6. Two-part fence on
router table

7. Pilot on router bit
on router table

1. Fence attached to workpiece

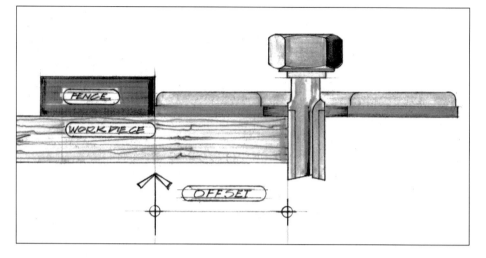

The **fence** is a piece of wood or a metal straight edge clamped onto the workpiece. The **guide** is the edge of the router base. The **offset** is the distance from the guide to the router bit's **cutting circle**.

This is the simplest and most common guide method. With it you can:

— Square the edge of the workpiece by taking a full cut with a straight bit.

— Make a rebate with a straight bit.

— Mold all or part of the edge with a curved or complex bit.

— Make a groove along the face of the workpiece. A fixed-base router can only make a through groove, while a plunge router can make a stopped groove.

— Make a dado or housing across the face of the workpiece. A fixed-base router makes a through housing, while a plunge router can make a housing that stops short of the edge of the wood.

— Make a mortise using a straight bit, a plunge router, and a simple jig.

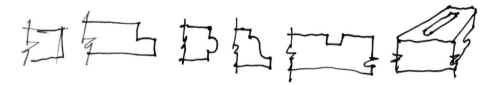

Square the edge of the workpiece by taking a full cut with a straight bit.

Make a mortise using a straight bit, a plunge router, and a simple pocket jig.

Rout a dado or housing across the workpiece.

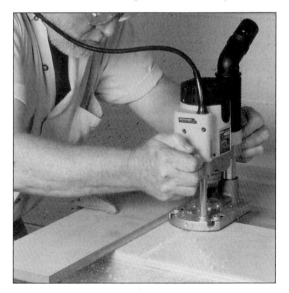

2. Base guide attached to router base

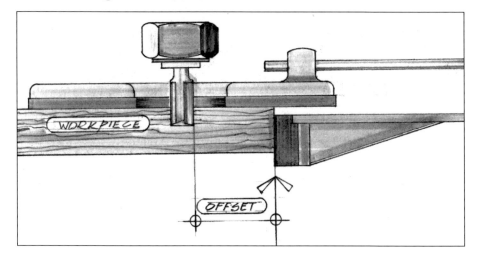

The **base guide** attached to the router base steers the router along the edge of the workpiece. The **fence** is the edge of the workpiece. The **offset** is the distance from the guide to the bit's **cutting circle**.

With this guide method you can:

— Mold part of a square edge, though not the whole edge, because part of it must remain intact to act as the fence.

—Run grooves, flutes, or decorative shapes parallel to the edge of the workpiece.

— Mold part of the edge of a circle, using a two-point version of the base guide.

— Flatten a surface, using an extended version of the router base.

— Rout a circle using a trammel that attaches to the router base like the regular base guide.

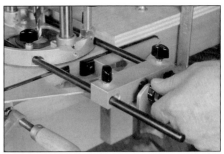

Adjusting the base guide

Mold part of a square edge, though not the whole edge, because part of it must remain intact to act as the fence.

Flatten a surface, using an extended version of the router base.

Rout a circle using a trammel that attaches to the router base like the regular base guide.

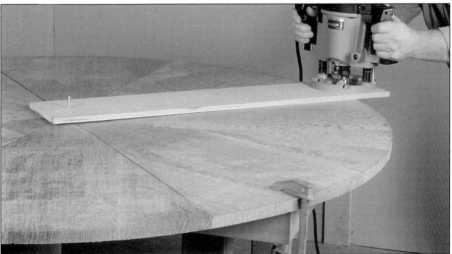

3. Pilot on router bit

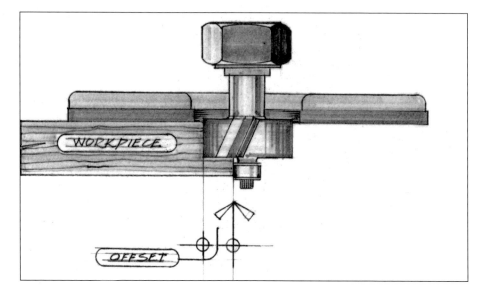

The solid pilot or ball-bearing pilot runs against the workpiece edge. The **guide** is the pilot bearing. The **fence** is the workpiece edge. The **offset** is the distance from the bearing's outer diameter to the **cutting circle**.

When the workpiece edge is the fence, the bearing can only shape part of the edge. The rest of the edge must remain untouched, or the cut would go out of control.

With this guide method you can:

— Make a rebate. One way to adjust the size of the rebate is to change the diameter of the bearing on the bit.

— Mold part of the edge of a board.

— Rout a groove or slot in the edge of a board.

— Rout multi-part shapes, such as the two-part pencil mold.

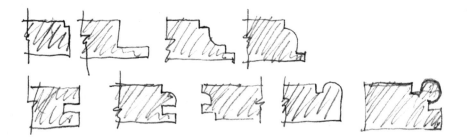

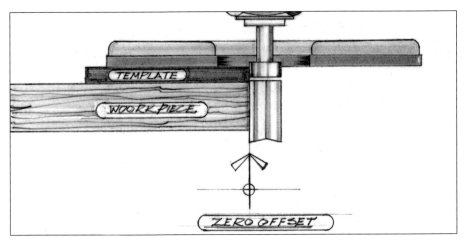

When a template is the fence, the bit can remove all or part of the workpiece edge. It's possible to construct equivalent setups with shank-mounted or tip-mounted bearings. However, when you're driving the router on top of the workpiece, you'll get the best view of what's happening with the template on top and a shank-mounted bearing.

When the offset is zero, this setup reproduces the shape of the template. This is the most accurate way to reproduce a curved or complex shape. It is how most dovetail jigs work.

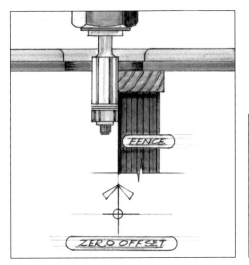

There's a hybrid situation when a bit with a tip-mounted bearing trims plastic laminate or a wood lipping flush with the adjacent surface. The bearing is the guide, the adjacent surface is the fence.

4. Guide Collar on router base

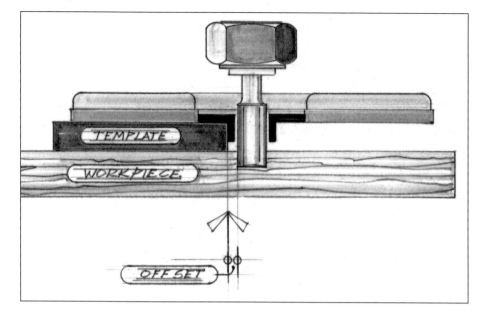

The guide collar is, in effect, a much reduced router base. It runs against a template. The **guide** is the outer surface of the collar. The **fence** is the template. The **offset** is the distance from the outside of the guide collar to the bit's **cutting circle**.

With this guide method you can:

— Make practically any shape recess or hole in or through a board.

— Cut the edge of a board straight.

— Rout a curve into the edge of a board.

— Make a rebate or a groove parallel to the edge of the template.

— Make an inlay and a matching recess in the wood.

This setup works well for straight cuts. When you use guide collars with a shaped template, the template has to be adjusted to compensate for the offset. Adding and subtracting offsets from templates is a source of much confusion, and most people have to experiment before they understand how it works. Nevertheless, it's often the only way to rout a recess that will exactly fit an inlay. More on page 80.

Cut the edge of a board straight.

Make an inlay and a matching recess in the wood.

Make a rebate or a groove parallel to the edge of the template.

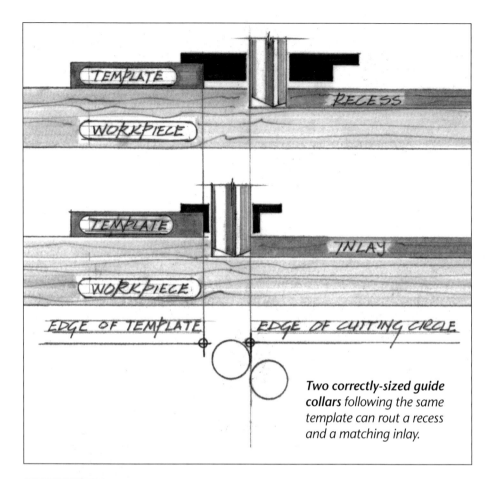

Two correctly-sized guide collars following the same template can rout a recess and a matching inlay.

Routing for inlays

Measure the guide collar with a dial caliper.

A guide collar can reproduce the shape of a template, reduced or enlarged by the offset distance between the outside of the collar and the bit's cutting circle. To rout an inlay and the recess it fits into, you need two different-sized guide collars. The size relationship is:

Outside Diameter of large collar -minus bit diameter

= equals Outside Diameter small collar +plus bit diameter.

For example, with a 1/2-inch bit, this combination works:

2-inch OD collar - 1/2-inch bit = 1-1/2 in.

1-inch OD collar + 1/2-inch bit = 1-1/2 in.

Similarly, with a 1/8-inch bit:

3/4-inch OD collar - 1/8-inch bit = 5/8 in.

1/2-inch OD collar + 1/8-inch bit = 5/8 in.

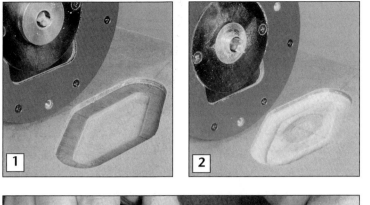

Fitting an inlay. *Using the same template, the large collar routs the recess (1) and the small collar routs the inlay (2).*

The inlay fits *neatly into its space (3).*

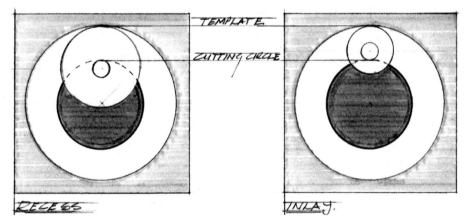

TEMPLATE

CUTTING CIRCLE

RECESS

INLAY.

Plan view shows the relatonship between guide collars, template, recess, and inlay.

It's a trade-off

Deciding whether to use a guide collar or a bit with a shank-mounted bearing is a trade-off. The bearing-guided bit reproduces the exact shape of the template in the workpiece, with no need to calculate offsets. However, it doesn't allow you to control the depth of cut, making the method impractical for most inlay work. While guide collars require an offset calculation, they give you control over the depth of the cut.

5. One-part fence on router table

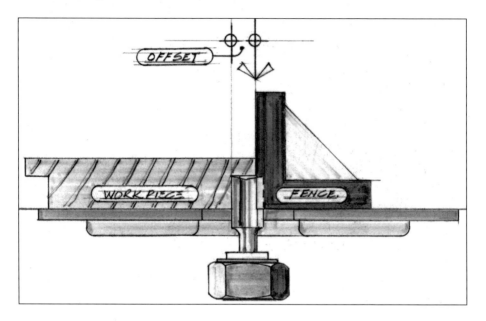

The **guide** is the edge of the workpiece. It runs against the router-table **fence**. The cutter is partially buried in the fence. The **offset** is the distance from the fence to the edge of the **cutting circle**.

When it's possible to make the cut you want with a one-part fence on the router table, it is the safest and simplest method of routing.

This method is accurate for cuts that do not remove the entire edge of the workpiece. If the cutter were to remove the entire edge of the workpiece, it would also destroy the guide surface, and the setup would be thrown out of control.

Work-holding sleds with fences that run on the front edge of the router table use the same guide method (page 124).

With a one-part fence on the router table you can:

— Rebate an edge.

— Mold part of an edge.

— Slot or groove the workpiece.

Note that you can use pilot-bearing bits with the router table fence, by setting the fence in line with the bearing or any-where forward of it.

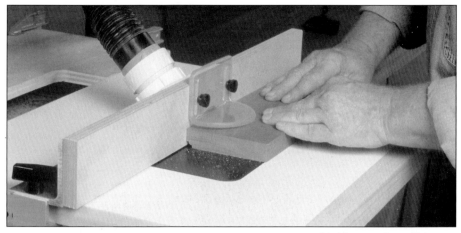

Mold part of an edge.

 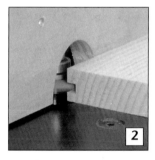

Rebate an edge (1).

Slot or groove the workpiece (2).

Mold using the fence instead of the bit's pilot bearing (1).

Panel raising is molding an edge (2).

Work-holding sleds with fences that run on the front edge of the router table are equivalent to fence-guided setups.

6. Two-part fence on router table

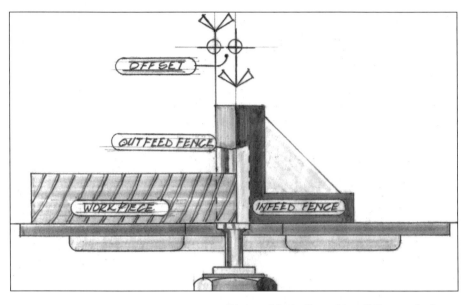

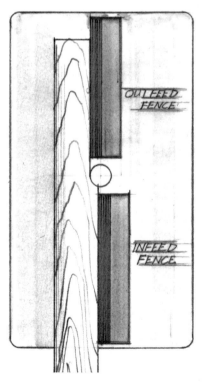

The **guide** is the edge of the workpiece. It runs against the two-part router-table fence. The cutter is partially buried in the **infeed fence**. The **offset** is the distance from the infeed fence to the **cutting circle**. The **outfeed fence** is aligned with the cutting circle.

A two-part fence is necessary any time you want to remove the entire edge of the workpiece. This is the situation, for example, when you are using the router table to prepare a face edge. The original, uncut portion of the workpiece edge bears against the infeed fence. The newly cut portion of the workpiece edge bears against the outfeed fence. The outfeed fence must be set forward by the exact depth of cut, that is, by the offset. The illustration shows how this works. The example on page 54 shows how to set the fences.

With this guide method you can:

— Remove all of an edge.

— Mold all of an edge.

Straightening an edge with the two-part router table fence

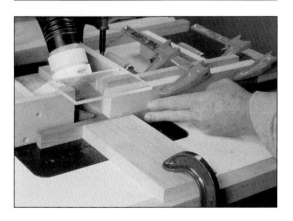

Molding the full edge with the two-part router table fence

Running molding strips with a guide tunnel on the two-part router table fence

7. Pilot on router bit on router table

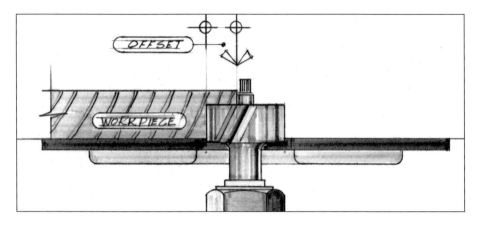

The pilot bearing is the **guide**. The **fence** is the workpiece edge, or a template attached to the workpiece. The **offset** is the distance from the outside of the pilot bearing to the **cutting circle**. This setup always requires a starting pin (page 52).

When the fence is the workpiece edge, this setup can mold a portion of the edge but it cannot remove all of it.

With this method you can:

— Make a rebate. One way to adjust the size of the rebate is to change the bearing on the bit.

— Mold part of the edge of a board.

— Rout a groove or slot in the edge of a board.

— Make cope-and-stick frames for cabinet doors.

— Raise a panel.

The pilot bearing guides the panel-raising bit, left, and the molding bit, below.

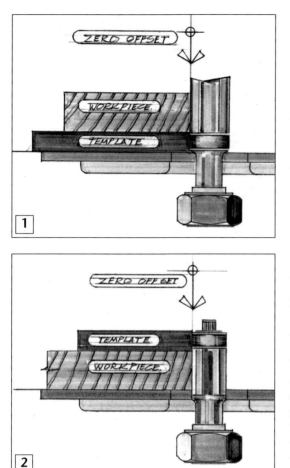

To shape the full edge of the workpiece, you must use a separate template. The template can be mounted on top of the workpiece or below it.

1. Mounting the template below the workpiece allows the edge of a work-holding sled to act as the template. This makes a safe and stable setup for pattern-routing shaped parts, such as chair legs.

2. Mounting the template on top of the workpiece gives you better visibility of the contact between guide and bearing. This calls for a bit with a tip-mounted pilot.

When the pilot bearing is the same size as the router bit, the offset is zero and the setup reproduces the template. When the pilot bearing is not the same size as the router bit, the offset reduces or enlarges the template profile.

The edge of the work-holding sled is the template. It's below the workpiece and works with a shank-mounted pilot.

The top-mounted template runs on a tip-mounted pilot bearing. This setup has good visibility.

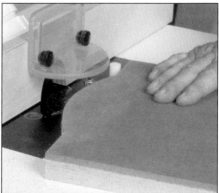

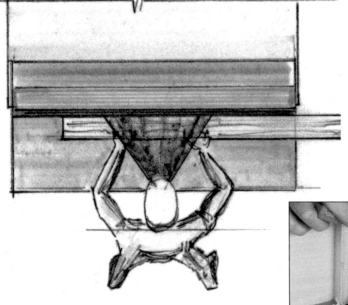

When the chips start to fly, keep both hands on the router or on the workpiece. Let your vision rove over the setup, but concentrate on the contact between workpiece and fence.

Chapter Seven

The Chips Fly

In every routing operation, once the chips start flying, many factors determine the safety and accuracy of the cut. They include:

The operator:

Hand position,

Grip,

Stance,

View.

The router:

Motor power,

Rotation speed,

Router heft.

The workpiece:

Clamp it,

Move it,

Wood density.

The chips fly:

Stability,

Cutting volume,

Direction of cut,

Rate of feed.

Don't cut the cord

When you're steering the router over the workpiece, it's very easy to catch the power cord on some part of the setup, so it suddenly snubs the operation. If you are concentrating on the line of cut, you might not realize what has happened, so you push harder. At best you might just pull the plug, but it's more likely you will upset the whole thing.

A variation on this calamity is routing through the cord, with sparks, smoke, and popped breakers.

The way to avoid both problems is to **rehearse the full path** before you switch the router on. Many woodworkers drape the power cord over one shoulder. This keeps it under control and out of the way.

Pull the plug

Before you attempt to change cutters you must pull the electrical plug. Anything might happen while you wrestle with wrenches stuck into the mechanism. Take no chances. Pull the plug.

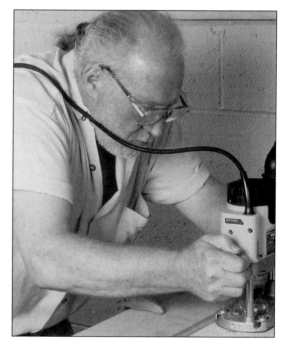

Freehand routing?

While it's barely possible to use the router freehand, there's no possibility of accuracy. The machine is simply too difficult to control. While you might imagine that you can freehand through a large area of waste inside a routed perimeter, you quickly run out of surface area to support the machine. The router is not a freehand tool.

The operator

More than anything else, successful routing depends upon a calm and clear-headed operator who has taken the time to understand the problem and to devise a thorough solution. It's your total responsibility to prepare the setup and make the cut without hurting yourself or any bystanders.

Hand position: When holding the router, keep both hands on the handles. One-handed routing is neither safe nor accurate. Pay attention to which way you twist the router. For example, a molding setup isn't stable when both your hands are in line with the edge of the workpiece. The same setup stabilizes if you just turn the router 90 degrees, so one handle moves onto the workpiece.

When feeding the workpiece over the router table, hold it with both hands and make sure both hands remain 6 inches (15cm) away from the cutter throughout the operation. Protecting your hands often requires making a fixture to hold the workpiece. The fixture may be as simple as a pair of toggle clamps and a stop block screwed onto an MDF sled.

Stance: Stand easy, with your feet positioned to direct the push and with your body balanced. Stand close to the center of the setup. By over-reaching from one end or the other, you risk losing your balance, inviting a mishap.

View: Cultivate a roving eye to ensure that everything proceeds as it should. At the same time, constantly return your attention to the point of contact between guide and fence. This is what ensures the success of the operation, and it is where

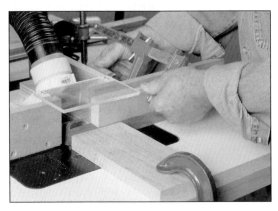

Jigs, clamps, and blocks allow you to drive the workpiece into the cutter without feeding it your fingers as well.

things most commonly go wrong. Usually you can see the contact point, and even when you can't, you will feel it. Focusing on the cut itself is not much help. You can't see anything through the cloud of chips. What's going on between the cutter and the wood results entirely from the setup, with guide-to-fence contact at the heart of it.

Preparation: You not only make the setup, but you also make or confirm a number of decisions on the fly, at the moment of switching the router on. In advance of switching on, you should rehearse the operation with the router switched off to make sure nothing hangs up and the cut will go as planned.

Sometimes woodworkers are reluctant to rehearse before the chips fly. I've never understood this reluctance — golfers, dancers, and musicians rehearse, why not woodworkers? If you take the time to think it through and rehearse, you'll prevent inaccurate cuts and you'll avoid dangerous errors.

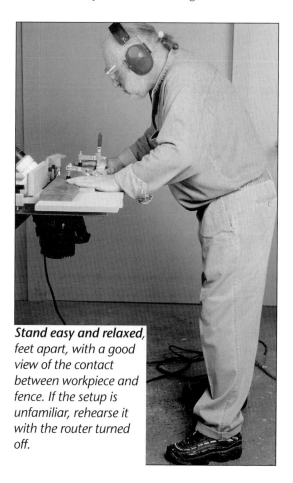

Stand easy and relaxed, feet apart, with a good view of the contact between workpiece and fence. If the setup is unfamiliar, rehearse it with the router turned off.

The machine

The size and configuration of the router should match the job at hand. For example, for mortising, a plunge router is the tool to use, not a fixed-base router, whereas for table routing most woodworkers prefer the fixed-base machine. While there is a lot of room for variation, you can't hog out a deep mortise with a little trim router, nor can you chamfer by balancing a 3 HP monster on the edge of the workpiece.

Motor power is less of a factor than woodworkers commonly believe. This is because the operator can compensate for an underpowered router by reducing both the feed rate and the volume of the cut.

Rotation speed can be varied on most modern plunge routers, which allows you to compensate for a large diameter cutter by slowing it down. There is no "correct" speed.

Router heft has a lot to do with how easy it is to control the cut. A heavy router will be more stable and less prone to vibration. One that is too heavy for the operator's physique will be difficult to manage.

The workpiece

The router's great virtue is versatility. This means there is very little that is constant from one workpiece to the next. Even so, the following general considerations apply:

Clamp it. If the workpiece is clamped to the bench, with the router traveling, then it cannot be responsible for any disintegration of the setup. You must make sure the workpiece is clamped firmly, and that it remains secure during the cut.

Move it. When the router is mounted in a table and the workpiece travels, its mass becomes a critical factor. A large workpiece helps keep the operator's hands away from the cutter. The mass of the wood adds to your strength, making it easier to overcome the cutting resistance.

A large workpiece has both size and mass. A small workpiece should be clamped to a hefty jig. This is why seasoned woodworkers make big, heavy work-holding jigs for routing.

Grain direction. Wood isn't plastic. Unlike plastic, it's not the same in all directions, it has a fibrous structure called grain. It's easier to cut the wood with the grain than across the grain. However, a rotating bit always cuts with the grain part of the time and against it part of the time. No matter how you arrange the setup, some part of the cut will lift the grain and leave a rough surface, called tear-out. You can minimize tear-out by taking a light cut, and you can remove it with a fine climb cut (page 96).

Wood density governs cutting volume. When routing light, low-density softwoods, the limiting factor is likely to be how well the bit clears itself of chips. When routing hard, dense woods, the limiting factor is likely to be the strength of the steel in the bit, and the power of the router motor. There are no hard-and-fast rules, beyond common sense. If the router lugs, if the bit chatters, if it packs up with chips and overheats, slow down or take a smaller bite.

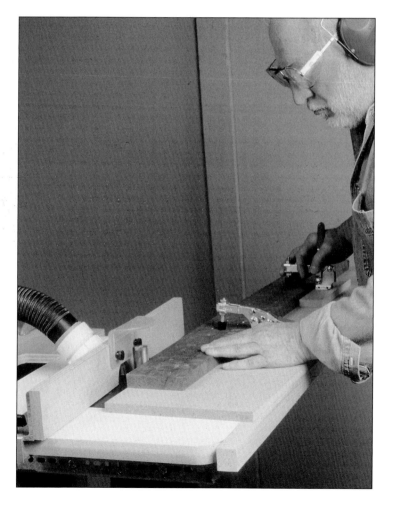

A hefty workpiece, here clamped to a heftier sled, takes a lot of uncertainty out of routing. It's always better to shape small parts on the edge of larger ones, then saw them apart after routing.

The chips fly

Finally you have chosen the router cutter and made the tightest, most accurate setup you can. You switch on the router. There's a lot of noise, the cutter meets the wood, and the chips start to fly. Immediately you will be dealing with the following:

Stability

As you steer the router into the wood, the cutting action begins to push back, and a setup that seemed right suddenly feels very unstable. Don't try to stabilize it on the fly. Switch off and figure out what's happening. It's especially difficult to steer the router along the narrow edge of a board. You may need to add a support block to the setup, or you may decide it would be better to switch from a router-on-top situation to the router table.

Stability. When you're routing an edge, an offset base puts more of the action over the workpiece. When you have to stand the wood up on edge, clamp a support block to it.

Cutting volume

The router makes a fine cut better than a heavy cut. Whenever you can remove the bulk of the waste wood by some other means, do so. For example, when you want to rout to a template, or make a round table top from a square piece of wood, bandsaw or jigsaw the waste wood first, then finish the cut with the router. When making mortises, drill out the bulk of the waste, staying about 1/16 inch (1.5 mm) inside the line. Sawing off the bulk of the waste makes the router operation less stressful and more accurate.

Cutting volume translates into cut resistance. Your decision depends on your own strength; on the bit design, diameter, and sharpness; on the hardness of the wood, and on the feed speed. A small roundover bit operating on an edge encounters very little cut resistance. A deep mortise in hardwood has tremendous cut resistance. The solution is to take the cut in stages — and you have to learn through experience how much to take in one bite. As a rule, with a 1/2-inch (12mm) bit I would not go deeper than 1/2 inch in a single pass.

The router is a finishing tool. When there's a lot of waste, saw most of it off before you rout.

Feed direction

When you look down on an upright router, the motor rotates clockwise. In every router setup, there are two choices for which way you feed the router into the workpiece:

Against the direction of rotation, called **aggressive cutting**,

With the direction of rotation, called **climb-cutting**.

In almost every situation, feed against the direction of rotation. This is called **aggressive cutting**. The cutting forces pull the router against the fence or template, and the operator must push against the router's force.

Feeding with the direction of rotation, or **climb-cutting**, immediately reveals our human strength, or lack of it. What would be a normal cutting volume as an aggressive cut runs away from you at a frightening speed as a climb-cut. The bit climbs over the wood like a wheel and runs out of control.

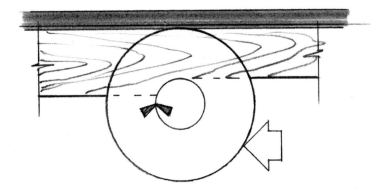

Feed direction. Whether you are driving the router (above) or the workpiece (below), the key is to make the cutter rotation push the workpiece onto the fence.

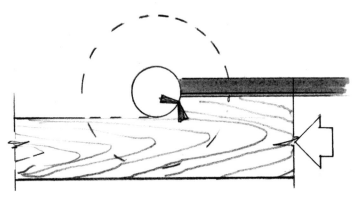

Nevertheless, climb-cutting can clean up a torn surface, but the cut volume must be tiny. To climb-cut safely, remove the bulk of the waste by normal, aggressive cutting, then clean up by removing the last 1/16 inch (1mm) or less with a climb-cut.

Climb-cutting requires some experience. Don't try it until you are comfortable with aggressive cutting, then practice on a spare workpiece. Just remove a whisker of wood, and always stay under 1/16 inch (1mm).

When you're plowing a groove in the face of the workpiece, one side of the bit will be cutting aggressively, while the other side will be climb-cutting. Resolve the apparent contradiction by traveling in the aggressive-cut direction along the fence.

It's not always obvious which way will be against the direction of rotation. The diagrams show how to figure it out. If your router doesn't have a visible arrow on the top of the housing to show its clockwise direction of rotation, paint one there.

Rate of feed

How fast to feed the cutter into the workpiece is almost entirely a matter of feel. If you go too fast, the chips won't clear, and the cut will become rough before it bogs down completely. If you go too slow, the cutter is liable to scorch the wood. The correct feed speed is the sweet spot the middle, and you will know it the first time you find it.

Power carving

Although some people use a router motor with a carving burr for power carving, it's the wrong tool for the job. The router simply runs too fast, so the burr clogs and glazes over. Get a right-angle die grinder or auto-body grinder instead. It runs slower, so the burr has a chance to clear its chips, and it's got a side handle so you can control it.

Sled jig works like a miter gauge. A straight rail glued to the front edge of the router table guides the jig's front fence. A simple sled like this is a good platform for more complex jigs.

Chapter Eight

Six Jig-Making Principles

Jigs for router operations have flooded the woodworking marketplace, and plans for them spill out of books and magazines. Each jig seems to be more elaborate than the one before, so that without a common understanding of fundamental principles, the whole subject quickly becomes a deep and expensive bog. In this chapter I'll attempt to lay down principles for designing and making router jigs.

My basic point of view is that jigs and setups should be simple, quick to make from stock materials and basic parts, and tailored to each new situation as the need arises. These jigs can be clamped together, screwed together, or both. This approach produces jigs that are designed for the task at hand They usually work better than elaborate or universal contraptions. When the job is done, the setup comes apart and the clamps go back on the rack.

The two fundamental situations — router on top, router in table — govern your jig-making strategy. Although the details of designing jigs differ according to whether the operator drives the router or the workpiece, the following six principles remain the same:

1. Stability. The jig has to be stable and tight. Once the cut begins, there's no time for teetering routers and shifting parts.

2. Accuracy. The jig has to deliver accurate contact between the router's guide surface and the fence or template, or it cannot guide the cut.

3. Constraint. The jig and fence have to constrain the path of the router or workpiece, so it goes only where you intend it to go and can't cut into wood you don't want to touch.

4. Rigidity. The jig parts must not deflect under the stress of the operation.

5. Economy. The jig must be easy, inexpensive, and straightforward to make.

6. Safety. The jig must not only keep the workpiece and everything else from flying loose, it must also keep the operator's fingers 6 inches (15cm) to 9 inches (24cm) away from the cutter.

I'll develop these six points using the example of a commonly available commercial dovetail jig, shown in the photo at left. By examining it closely, you'll see these six principles unfold. I'll extend the same points to the shop-made bracket jig, set up for edge-mortising in the photo at right. You'll see this jig being put together in the next chapter.

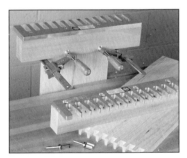

The Kellar dovetailing jig, above, illustrates the six principles of jig making, and so does the shop-made bracket jig.

Stability

Stability depends on the geometry of the setup and on the jig-making materials. In the dovetail jig, the workpiece is clamped in the vise, then the jig is clamped to the workpiece. The length of the fingers and the width of the aluminum plate keep the router base fully supported throughout the cut.

Many standard operations have stability problems. When molding an edge, more than half of the router base extends beyond the surface of the workpiece. You can stabilize it with an offset base plate or a supplementary support block under the router base (see page 94).

Moving to the router table shifts the problem of stability from the router to the workpiece. It's solved when you can lay the workpiece flat on the table surface. When the workpiece must stand up on edge, use the high fence (page 52).

Stability of another kind is the key criterion for choosing jig materials. You need materials that come flat from the store and stay flat when you cut and join them — as do MDF, Masonite, Lexan and aluminum. Plywood is good in small pieces, but large pieces unfortunately tend to twist. Solid wood moves in response to changing humidity. Large, solid-wood support blocks may be square the day you make them, but might not remain square as the seasons change. Check them and correct them as necessary.

Stability. When clamped to the workpiece and held in the vise, the dovetail jig, left, provides the router with a stable platform. The bracket jig, above, set up for end mortising, acquires stability from the bench and vise.

Accuracy

Accuracy depends on the fence and the guide edge. In the dovetail jig, the aluminum plate is the fence, and the shank-mounted bearing is the guide surface. Both have been machined with precision. In clamp-and-block setups, accuracy depends on how well you make and position the fence on which the guide surface runs.

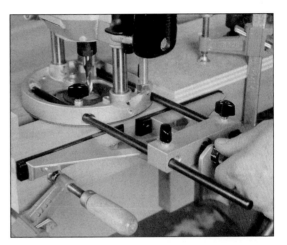

Accuracy. Machined slots precisely fit the pilot bearing, above. The router's base guide, right, has a screw for precise adjustment.

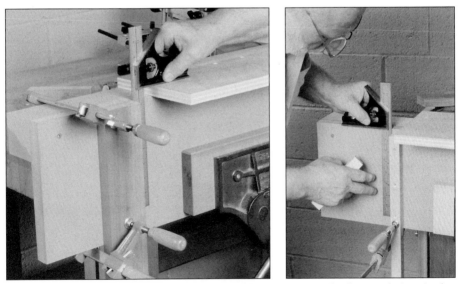

Accuracy with clamps and blocks: Locate the first workpiece in the bracket jig, then clamp or screw a stop tightly against it to position the rest of the workpieces. Accuracy depends on cutting the jig parts square and assembling them squarely.

Constraint

On the tail-making half of the dovetail jig, the slots exactly fit the shank-mounted guide bearing on the router bit. The jig constrains the bit's motion in three directions, which leaves the fourth direction unconstrained so the bit can enter the workpiece. The part that makes the pins constrains a zero-offset straight bit that makes a void into which the tail exactly fits.

In most setups, the operator achieves constraint in two directions by pressing the router down on the workpiece or the workpiece down on the router table, and the guide surface against the fence. However, there is nothing to stop the router from moving away from the fence. When the bit is cutting on one side only, as when molding an edge, it doesn't matter. Deviation means only that it cuts into the air, not into the wrong part of the workpiece, and a second pass puts the cut right. However, when the objective is a groove, a mortise, or a housing, it's critical to constrain both sides of the cut with a fence on each side.

Stop blocks aren't necessary for cuts that proceed from one end of the workpiece to the other, but they're critical when you want the cut to begin and end in exactly the right place.

Constraint. Milled slots determine exactly where the dovetail bit can cut and where it can't. Stop blocks clamped in place do the same job on the bracket jig.

Rigidity

All attention to accuracy and constraint goes out the window if the fence or guide surface deflects under cutting load, or under the pressure exerted by the operator. In the dovetail jig, rigidity comes from screwing the 3/8-inch (9mm) thick aluminum plate to a heavy wooden support rail, making a T-shaped section that resists load from every direction.

The heft of the router, of the fence, and of the workpiece all play an important part in making a setup rigid. This is why it's critical to clamp the workpiece to the bench, or to hold it in a vise. It's why small parts have to be clamped to a hefty jig before they can be fed across the router table. It's also why soft rubber mats are not adequate platforms for accurate routing.

Rigidity. Screws lock the dovetail jig's aluminum top plate onto the wooden support rail, and clamps tie it to the vise-held workpiece.

The bracket jig consists of two MDF plates screwed to a stout support rail. The jig relies on the rigidity and stability provided by the workbench and vise.

Economy

Economy is the underlying factor in every design problem. In jig-making, economy includes the cost of materials, construction time and effort, setup time and effort, and storage between uses. Economical jigs are quick and straightforward to make.

Many woodworkers, no doubt encouraged by magazines, are convinced that elaborate, universally adjustable jigs featuring tee nuts, plastic knobs, springs, and aluminum fences are the norm. It's not the case. Elaborate jigs take a lot of time and fuss to make, which I've never found economical. Also, universal jigs tend to be large and unwieldy, and usually they are not quite what you really need for each particular task. You are better off developing a basic vocabulary of jig-making skills and techniques. This makes it easy for you to tailor a new jig to each new situation.

Compare the example jig, which makes dovetails in a limited range of sizes, with universal dovetailers. One is simple and straightforward to understand. The other has an owner's manual the size of a computer handbook.

You may object that the example jig was purchased, not made in the shop. But that's precisely the point: While it's possible to make a jig as accurate and long-lasting as this one, it would cost a lot of time and money.

You can use the six jig-making principles to assess any commercially manufactured jig. Some of them will succeed on every point. They're probably worth purchasing. Others fail on most points, and they probably are not worthwhile.

Economy. The box joint jig, left, which makes an excellent case joint, consists of an MDF fence screwed to a Masonite sled. The dado jig, above, is even simpler.

Safety

A correct setup — where the router and workpiece are stable, rigid, accurate, and constrained — is a safe setup. Achieving these attributes also confers a certain size to the jig or setup, which allows the operator to get a grip 6 inches (15cm) to 9 inches (22cm) away from the cutting action. In the example dovetail jig, both the operator's hands must be on the router handles, well out of the cutting path.

In situations where the router moves, the jig has to be clamped in the vise or to the workbench, the workpiece has to be clamped to the jig, and the operator has to keep both hands on the machine. The setup is safe.

When the workpiece moves over the router table, it's important to make the parts large and heavy. The heft of the setup adds to the operator's strength, and the size of the setup keeps the operator's fingers away from the cutting action.

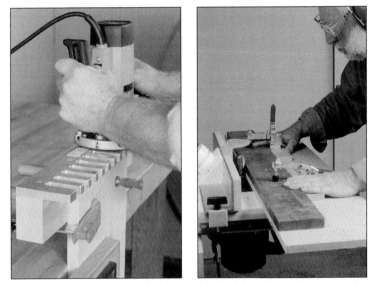

Safety. A stable routing platform, with both hands on the router, is a safe setup. On the router table, a hefty jig helps keep control of the setup, and also keeps your hands away from the bit.

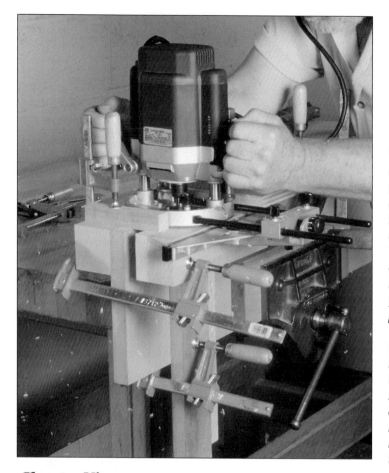

Thicket of clamps. It takes four clamps to adapt the bracket jig for end mortising. The setup looks complicated, but it's not, as you'll see on page 118.

Clamps and blocks tailor the jig to any size workpiece and any mortise layout, making the jig truly universal.

Chapter Nine

Making and Using Router Jigs

Although many kinds of jigs are suitable for the router, you'll find you can get a lot of mileage from just five. Four of them rely on the bench and vise, and one is for the router table. The five jigs are:

T-square jig,

Pocket jig,

Bracket jig,

Saddle jig,

Sled jig (router table).

In this chapter I'll step through the construction, loading, and operation of each of these jigs, along with a number of important variations on them.

Five basic jigs

T-square jig for housings (page 111)   *Pocket jig* for mortising (page 112)

Saddle jig for tenoning (page 114)

Basic jigs can be adapted to almost any routing problem. These economical jigs securely hold the workpiece, provide a stable platform for routing, guide the router, and stop the cut.

Bracket jig for mortising (page 118)   *Sled jig* on the router table (page 122)

Clever setups are fun to figure out

The six jig-making principles of stability, accuracy, constraint, rigidity, economy, and safety should be applied to every setup. In this and the following chapter I'll describe procedures that have worked for me, and I'll analyze each one in terms of fence, guide surface, and offset, along with practical setup details. However, nowhere do I mean to suggest that these methods are the only methods. Part of the delight of woodworking is thinking up new and clever ways to do the job. The more you understand about your tools, materials, and setups, the more success you'll have.

Jig-making materials

In the woodworking industry, each jig is made for a single, specific purpose. It will only accept one size of workpiece and it makes only one cut or part — but it does its job many, many times. Industrial jigs are hefty and robust, they clamp the workpiece firmly, and they keep the operator's hands away from the cutter. They're an investment that pays out over a long period of use.

If you are not doing production work, you want all these same characteristics, except you don't need permanence or expense. The solution is to make jigs from blocks and plates of stable material, and instead of making them permanent with screws and glue, construct each setup by clamping the parts together.

It's most efficient and economical to construct each jig and setup as you need it, then take it apart when done. Many of the parts can be re-used for the next jig. This approach keeps the small shop from filling up with jigs that never will be used again. When you do come up with an effective jig, you can screw and glue the parts together to make it permanent.

You can make good jigs using the same materials as for regular woodworking. Like solid wood, any of the man-made boards can be glued up to make thick sections and substantial blocks. Here's a rundown on common materials from a jig-making perspective:

High density fiberboard (Masonite) comes in sheets that are 1/8 inch (3mm) or 1/4 inch (6mm) thick. Tempered Masonite is ideal for making patterns, which you then attach to the workpiece. A bit guided by a bearing will then cut the workpiece to the exact shape of the pattern. Masonite is hard enough to stand up to repeated use, and it's easier to cut and shape than aluminum or Lexan, which would be industry's choice.

Medium density fiberboard (MDF) comes in sheets from 1/4 inch (6mm) to 1 inch (25mm) thick. It's extremely flat and stable, and it stays flat as the humidity changes. Pieces of MDF can be glued together face to face, to make large blocks and rigid fences. The material holds screws on its faces, though not in its edges. Thus, when you need to join it edge-to-face, it's best to insert a solid-wood glue block. You can screw through the glue block into the faces of both pieces of MDF.

Particle board has similar characteristics to MDF; it's sold in two grades, construction and industrial, with industrial having smoother faces and altogether higher specifications. **Plywood** comes in sheets 1/4 inch (6mm) to 1 inch (25mm) thick. It has smooth surfaces and edges, and excellent screw-holding ability on both face and edge. However, plywood frequently twists during manufacturing and stays that way afterward. To eliminate distortion, you have to cut it into relatively small pieces, so it's useful in jig-making.

Solid wood isn't the best material for permanent jigs because it tends to shrink, expand, and distort with seasonal changes in humidity. Normal wood movement is more than enough to destroy the accuracy of most setups. However, if you clamp each jig together for the task at hand, you don't have to worry about wood movement. Solid wood won't distort during the few hours or days it's involved in one of these jigs, though you may need to square it up before you reuse the same block in another jig.

Toggle clamps are a big help in holding the workpiece onto jigs, especially on the router table. The kind that screw onto the jig base are easy to position and remove, so they can be reused. An inventory of a half-dozen toggle clamps is more than enough.

Jig-making tools and supplies

You can cut and join jig parts with normal woodworking tools and supplies: glue, screws, and nails, depending on disassembly and design. I keep two cordless drills ready: one fitted with a combination bit for drilling countersunk clearance holes, and the other with a driver for Phillips (cross-head) or Robertson (square-drive) screws. If you've got compressed air in the shop, an air nailer is very helpful.

Clamps

Clamps are the key to making and using jigs. When you want to screw a fence to a jig platform, always clamp the two parts together before you drill pilot holes. When you want to locate a stop block on a jig, clamp the workpiece in position first, then clamp the stop block to it, then clamp or screw the stop block to the jig base.

There's a method to setting clamps. First, position the fixed head and level it on the work with one hand. Second, use your other hand to bring the movable head into contact with the setup, and to tighten the screw. It seems trivial but it makes all the difference.

Joining jig parts

Router jigs will be no more accurate than their component parts. Man-made sheet materials are stable and easy to cut and join with screws, provided you drill a clearance hole for the screw shank and a pilot hole for its threads. These materials tend to bulge outward when you drill through, so it's necessary to countersink on both sides.

Here's a general method for putting jig parts together. In this sequence I'm making a right-angle sled for the router table. This sled can be used exactly like a miter gauge on the table saw. It will carry the workpiece past the bit, and it makes a flat platform for a 45-degree fence (page 125) or for more complex jigs such as the box-joint jig (page 126).

Drill clearance holes *through the Masonite and countersink on both sides.*

Clamp the parts *in the right position. Check with your square and adjust as necessary.*

Drill pilot holes *into the wooden block. Don't skip this step.*

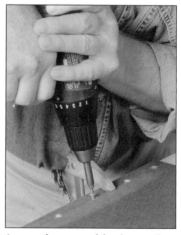

Leave the assembly *clamped together while you drive the screws down tight.*

A square connection

To make a square connection, tack the parts together with a single clamp, and use the square to align them.

Drill and drive the first screw. Remove the clamp, check for square and adjust, then reclamp to drill and drive the remaining screws.

T-Square jig for housings (dados)

The T-square jig guides the router for cutting dados or housings across the face of the workpiece. For accurate results, set up and join the two parts as shown on these pages. Using the jig for the first time makes a cutout in the cross piece, indicating the offset. Use this cutout to position the jig.

Pocket jig

A pocket jig makes a slot or pocket for the workpiece. Pocket jigs are especially good for routing mortises or grooves in square posts and legs. The showcase joint shown on this book's cover was made with a pocket jig, as described on the next page.

Build the jig on a baseboard of MDF or particleboard. Make the pocket with extra wood of the same dimension as the workpiece. Space the jig parts by clamping them to a workpiece, then screw the jig parts in place.

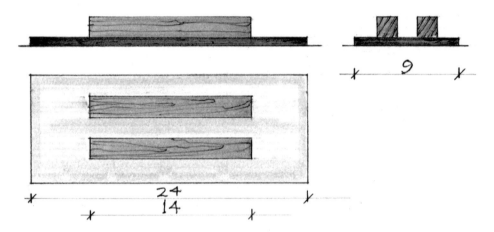

The pocket jig consists of two or four short lengths of leg stock screwed to a particleboard base. Space them with a workpiece. This makes a broad and stable routing platform.

Add fences to constrain the router's motion. Load a workpiece and plunge the router so you can see how the bit lines up with the layout. Clamp the fences and make a shallow test cut, then screw them in place.

Add a stop block to locate the end of the workpiece. Clamp the jig base to the workbench, set the depth of cut, and you're ready to rout.

Pocket jig for showcase joint

This version of the pocket jig routs mortises in the mitered faces of the three-way show-case joint. The miters were trimmed with a sled jig on the router table (page 133). Loose tenons complete the joint (page 143).

After routing, square up the rounded end of the slot with a chisel.

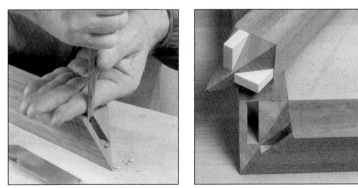

ig routs tenons

The saddle jig routs the faces and shoulders of tenons. The jig is quick to make, so you can tailor it to your current project. It works with a spiral end-mill and a guide collar.

Spiral end-mill with guide collar.

The jig indexes off the face side, long edges, and end of the workpiece. This means that the wood has to be prepared with a flat face side, with both ends square and to finished length, and with both long edges square and parallel.

The keys to accuracy:

1. Assemble the jig so the rail that indexes the workpiece is perfectly square to the guide edge of the larger platform. The photos on page 111 show how to do it.

2. To give the router a chance to cut all four tenon shoulders in the same plane, index the stop block off the square end of the workpiece. Unscrew the stop block to reposition it for different-length tenons.

3. Set up by clamping each workpiece to the jig and bench in the three-step sequence shown on page 116.

Make the rails from 24-inch (60cm) lengths of 5/8-inch x 5/8-inch (16mm x 16mm) wood, and this jig will handle parts between 5/8 inch (16mm) and 7/8 inch (22mm) thick. However, if you're making a cabinet with a number of doors, or a whole kitchen, it's best to make a new jig using extra door parts for the support rails. This ensures that the jig and workpiece sit tight on the workbench, flat and stable for routing. Note that this jig indexes from each end of the workpiece. For the between-shoulders distance to be right, all the workpieces have to be exactly the same length.

Saddle jig helps you rout precise tenons to fit any style of mortise.

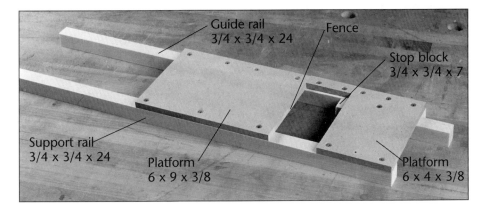

Guide rail
3/4 x 3/4 x 24

Fence

Stop block
3/4 x 3/4 x 7

Support rail
3/4 x 3/4 x 24

Platform
6 x 9 x 3/8

Platform
6 x 4 x 3/8

Making the saddle jig

Assemble the jig by screwing the platforms to the rails. The only critical connection is between the 6x9 platform and the guide rail. Make sure the fence edge of the platform is square to the guide rail, as shown on page 111.

Pare a chip clearance on the stop block. This beveled corner goes down, toward the bench.

To locate the stop block, position a test workpiece in the jig, and bring the block up to it. Clamp the stop block to the guide rail so you can screw it to the platform. When you set up the test piece, account for the offset distance from guide collar to cutting circle.

Loading the saddle jig

The saddle jig takes advantage of the flat workbench. If you clamp it to a surface that isn't flat, it probably won't make an accurate tenon. Here's the three-clamp maneuver.

1. Clamp the workpiece to the bench.

2. Clamp the jig rail to the workpiece, with the stop block tight against it.

3. Clamp the jig platform down tight on the workpiece.

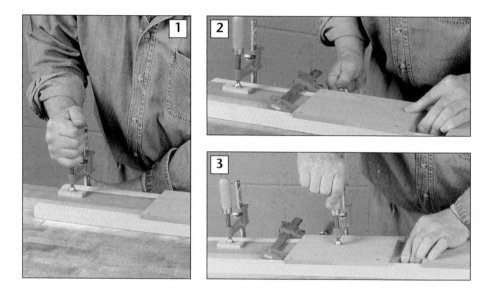

Slick tricks

The router should slide easily across the jig platform. Help it by sanding off any divots raised by drilling and counter-sinking. Then rub paraffin wax, or the end of a candle, into the surface and buff it with a rag.

Routing tenons with the saddle jig

Set the depth of cut by raising the bit against a small combination square. Check it by routing a test piece.

Rout to full depth with the guide collar pressed tightly against the edge of the jig platform. Then work back and forth to remove all the waste from the face of the tenon.

The same jig also can rout the side shoulder on the tenon.

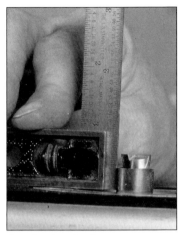

Set the depth of cut *by measuring from the router's base plate. Set the plunge router's depth stop.*

Chips expand *to three times the volume of the wood. Wear your safety glasses.*

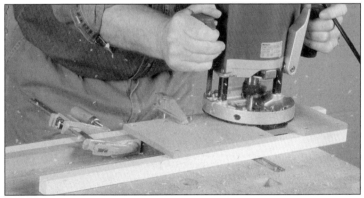

To rout the side shoulder, *clamp the jig to the edge of the workpiece, then trap workpiece and jig in the bench vise.*

Bracket jig

The bracket jig can mortise the edge, end, or face of the workpiece. It is quick and versatile. The top plate is the key to accuracy. Its edge is the routing fence. Clamping the workpiece beneath it automatically aligns the parts.

The basic idea is to screw the three-piece bracket together, then clamp stop blocks and support rails as needed. While you could replace the clamps with T-nuts and plastic knobs, such add-ons would cost money and time, and also would make the jig less versatile.

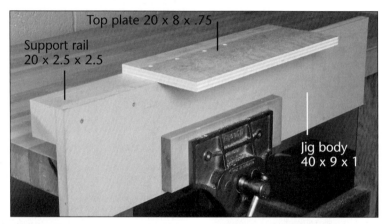

Top plate 20 x 8 x .75

Support rail
20 x 2.5 x 2.5

Jig body
40 x 9 x 1

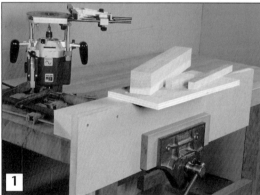

1. Clamp the jig in the bench vise. You'll also need a loose support rail, stop blocks, several clamps, and a side guide for the plunge router.

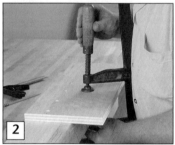

2. Clamp the workpiece to the jig's top plate. This guarantees alignment.

3. Draw a line across the jig that is the distance of the router's offset from the fence edge of the top plate. Index the mortise layout line to this offset line.

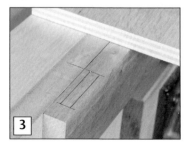

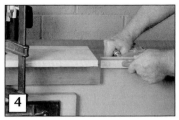

4. Clamp a stop block against the far end of the workpiece. It locates the wood when you reload the jig.

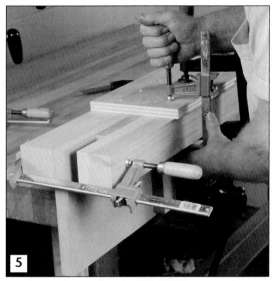

5. Clamp the support rail to the jig. One clamp indexes the rail against the top plate. The second clamp locks the rail and workpiece to the jig body

6. The last clamp positions the stop block that determines the length of the mortise.

7. Plunge the bit to the layout line and adjust the base guide to get the mortise in exactly the right place.

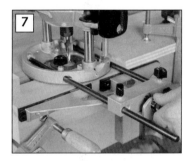

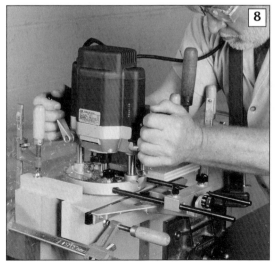

8. Now rout. Plunge to full depth at either end of the mortise, then come up to remove the waste with 1/2-inch (12mm) bites.

9. The completed mortise

Loading the bracket jig

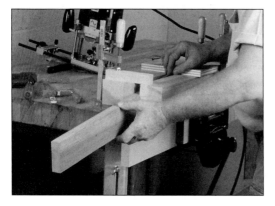

To reload the bracket jig, loosen the clamp that holds the support block against the top plate. Then remove the two clamps that trap the workpiece itself. Now you can slide the completed workpiece out and insert the next one. Replace two clamps and tighten one, and you're ready to rout on.

Mortise the workpiece face

The bracket jig makes it easy to mortise the face of the workpiece. The setup is simpler than for edge-mortising, because you don't need the support rail. Clamp the workpiece up against the jig's top plate, then clamp it against the jig body. Set end stops and adjust the side guide.

To mortise the face of the workpiece, clamp it to the jig's top plate and to the jig body.

The bracket jig and plunge router make an accurate mortise in the face of the workpiece.

End-mortising with the bracket jig

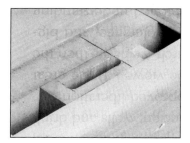

The bracket jig routs excellent mortises in the ends of the workpiece. This technique allows you to make matching mortises in the edge of one piece and in the end of the other. A loose tenon completes the joint.

The end-mortising setup uses exactly the same jig as edge-mortising, with the addition of a vertical stop screwed to the jig body.

Clamp the workpiece to the jig body. Get it square and in the right place by indexing the mortise layout to the offset line drawn on the jig body.

Clamp the vertical stop against the workpiece, then remove the workpiece. Check that the stop is square before you screw it to the jig body.

Clamp each workpiece against the vertical stop. Add the support rail and end stops, set the router's base guide, and rout.

Sled jig for straightening an edge

The sled is the simplest form of jig for the router table. The jig is nothing but a flat platform with one straight edge and with a couple of toggle clamps screwed to it. You clamp the workpiece to the platform, then guide the jig's straight edge against a shank-mounted bearing. This allows the router bit to work on the whole of the workpiece edge. A jig like this is most commonly used to put a straight edge on the workpiece — it makes the router table into an effective edge-jointer. It can mold the full edge with a curved bit, and it can be modified to reproduce a curved shape in the workpiece.

A sled jig, used with a straight bit that has a shank-mounted bearing, puts a straight edge on the workpiece. The router table fence acts as a top guard and dust port — it plays no role in guiding the cut.

The sled jig's heft keeps the operator's hands well away from the cutting action.

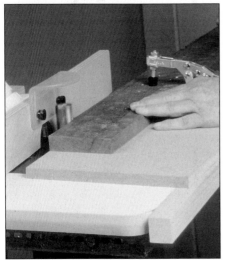

Sled jig for curved parts

You can make any kind of curved part using sled jigs: chair back legs and back splats, skirt rails, toy parts, plaques. This sled jig makes top rails for arch-top doors. The guide method is a shank-mounted ball-bearing pilot running on the edge of the sled itself. Jigs like this — which can include angled ramps and support blocks for complex parts — are quick to make. They are as accurate as the original template.

The principle of the sled jig is simple and universal: Make a totally stable platform, then anchor the blank workpiece to it using stop blocks and toggle clamps.

The difficult part of making curved parts is generating the pattern. It's easy when you start from an original part — you can use this same jig to rout a new pattern from the part. When you are starting from a drawing, you can jigsaw the pattern, file it, plane it, sand it, putty it with auto-body plastic, or beaver it with your sharp front teeth. Whatever your technique, when you want to make a smooth and regular workpiece, you have to generate a smooth and regular pattern.

1. Load the blank and trace its outline.

3. Reload and set the bit height.

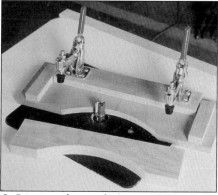

2. Remove the workpiece and jigsaw the bulk of the waste off it.

4. And rout.

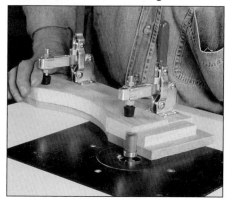

Sled with right-angle fence

This form of the sled jig is the router-table equivalent of a table saw miter gauge. It can be used to run a groove across the end of the workpiece. With a cope-and-stick cutter set, it will make the cope cut on the end of the rails for a cabinet door.

The jig consists of a square of 1/4-inch tempered Masonite with two fences attached to it. The bottom fence or guide fence runs along the front edge of the router table. The top fence, which is at right angles to the guide fence, locates the workpiece.

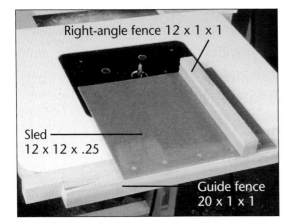

Right-angle fence 12 x 1 x 1

Sled
12 x 12 x .25

Guide fence
20 x 1 x 1

The right-angle sled jig guides along the front edge of the router table. It can make the cope cut for a cabinet door.

Set the depth of the cope cut by clamping a stop block to the router table fence. The workpiece must clear the stop block before it reaches the cutter. The router table fence also puts a top guard over the operation, and acts as a dust port.

Sled with miter fence

To make a sled jig for mitering, screw the top fence at a 45-degree angle to the guide fence. With a straight cutter, this setup will miter the end of a workpiece, such as the legs and rails of the showcase joint shown on this book's cover. With a slot cutter, it will make the slot for a splined miter joint, good for box lids and picture frames. Mitering exerts a lot of pressure on the workpiece, so clamp it to the jig fence.

Screw the 45-degree miter fence to the base of the sled jig. Clamp the workpiece to it.

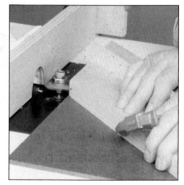

A slot cutter runs a groove in the mitered end of this frame piece.

This is a robust bit, but it can't chew a miter in one bite. Nibble in easy stages, or saw off the bulk of the waste before routing.

Sled for box joints

The right-angle sled jig is the platform for a box-joint jig. This jig works with stock of almost any width and thickness. The indexing key is a square stick the size of the router bit. It determines the width and spacing of the joint fingers. To use a different bit, make a new jig.

This is an example of a step-and-repeat jig, where the cut just made drops onto the key, thus indexing the next cut.

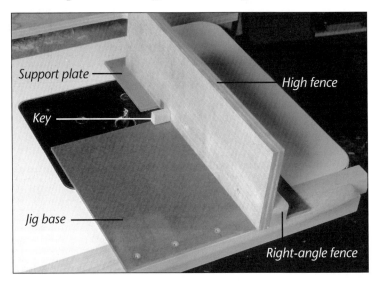

Support plate

Key

Jig base

High fence

Right-angle fence

2. Position the high fence on the right-angle fence so there is exactly one bit diameter between the key and the cutting circle of the router bit.

3. Screw the two fences together from the front.

1. Rout a bit-wide slot through the high fence and glue the key into it. Then screw the small support plate to the fence alongside the key.

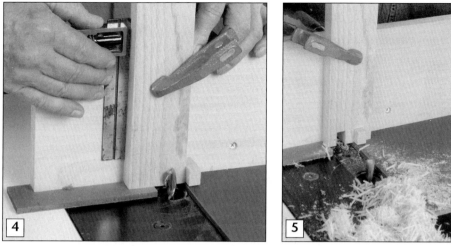

4. Clamp the workpiece to the jig, tight against the key. The square checks that it is vertical.

5. Rout the first slot, then fit the slot over the key and rout the next one. With a wide workpiece, continue across in the same way.

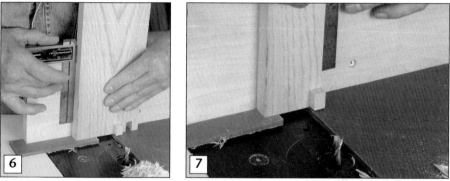

6. Since the first part of the joint begins with a finger, the second part must start with a space. Use one workpiece to position the other.

7. Fit the space over the key, and continue to rout across the width of the wood.

8. Test the fit of the joint. It should be snug. To adjust, tap the high fence one way or the other.

Straighten an edge

Mold all of an edge

Rebate

Mold part of an edge

Groove

Housing (dado)

Routers do many things, but they mostly come down to these six basic cuts. Changing their size and proportions gives you the elements of decorative moldings and joints for all kinds of furniture and general woodworking.

Chapter Ten
Catalog of Router Setups

The problem is how to cut the shape you want into the face, the edge, or the end of a piece of wood. The solution lies in the correct combination of router bit and setup. When you figure there are seven basic guide methods (page 71), and add to that all possible bit lengths, diameters, and profiles, it's clear that there are a staggering number of choices. This catalog gives you a variety of workable solutions to many typical problems. Once you grasp the logic of it, you'll become able to analyze which setup works best for the problem at hand and the equipment you have. You'll soon build your own vocabulary of techniques and jigs.

This catalog refers frequently to the **seven guide methods** in Chapter 6 (page 68), and the **five basic jigs** in Chapter 8 (page 98).

The catalog includes setups where the **operator drives the router** on top of the workpiece, as well as router-table setups where the **operator drives the workpiece**. In most cases, the router table is more stable, safer, and more accurate.

Straighten an edge

While the router is not a complete preparation tool, it can be used to create a straight edge, to trim an applied lipping flush with the face of the wood, and to flatten an irregular slab. Your setup has to be held firm with clamps or temporary screws.

Straighten an edge: fence on top

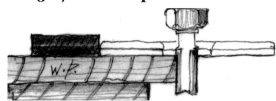

Guide the router base against a straight edge clamped to the workpiece. Rotate the machine to put one handle firmly over the contact between base and fence.

Straighten an edge: fence underneath

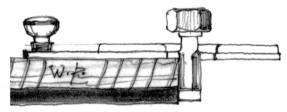

Guide a tip-mounted bearing against a straight fence that's under the workpiece. An offset base plate will help stabilize the router.

Straighten an edge: shank-mounted bearing

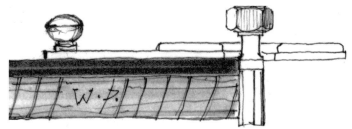

Guide a shank-mounted bearing against a straight fence that's on top of the workpiece. An offset base plate stabilizes the router.

Straighten an edge: template and guide collar

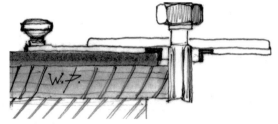

Guide the router with a collar that runs against a straight template; the offset is half the difference between the outside diameters of bit and collar. An offset base adds stability to the setup.

Straighten an edge: router table with split fence

Guide the workpiece against the split fence. A spiral bit leaves the smoothest surface; use the largest one you have. Set up the fence as on page 54.

Straighten an edge: router table with sled jig

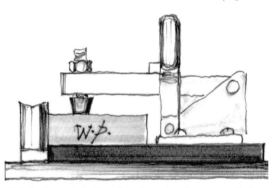

Guide the workpiece by clamping it onto a sled. Run the edge of the sled against a shank-mounted bearing. The sled has to be a couple of inches longer than the workpiece, and wide enough for toggle clamps. More on page 122.

Straighten and trim veneers

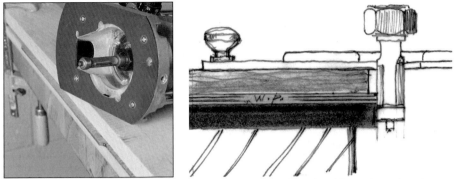

Clamp the veneers *between a straight-edged fence board and a second clamping board. Guide the router with a pilot bearing that rides on the edge of the fence board. With a shank-mounted bearing, the fence board goes on top; with a tip-mounted bearing, it goes on the bottom. Clamp the whole assembly so it overhangs the edge of the bench. An offset base plate improves stability.*

Straighten and trim veneers: router table

Trap the veneers *between a straight fence board and a second clamping board. Screw the clamping boards together; use a straight bit with a shank-mounted bearing.*

Trim the edge of a circle

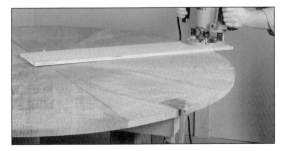

To trim a circle, *remove the regular base plate and screw the router to a plywood trammel. Saw the circle close to the line. Drill a hole to center the trammel on a nail or steel pin. Rout the circle smooth with a straight bit, or mold it with a shaped bit.*

Trim lippings and edgings

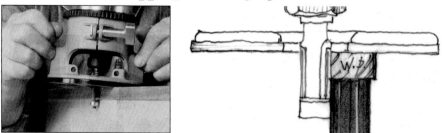

Guide the router with a tip-mounted bearing that runs along the face of the workpiece. Use a trim router, and turn the router so one of its handles allows stable pressure directly over the flat face of the lipping or edging. Too much glue will leave a hardened drool that interferes with the pilot bearing.

Trim lippings and edgings: router table

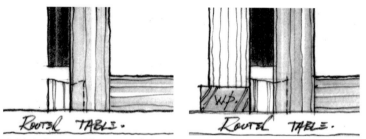

A high fence with an auxiliary plate supports the workpiece. Align the straight bit's cutting circle with the face of the auxiliary plate.

Flatten a slab

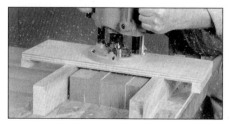

Screw the slab or burl to a an MDF base, tight between two rails. Replace the regular base plate with a plywood auxiliary base; make it twice as wide as the distance between the rails. Add stop blocks. Take the cut in easy bites and be ready to sweep up a lot of chips.

Trim a miter

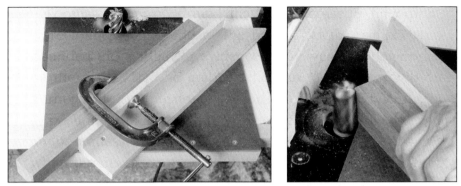

Clamp the workpiece to a sled with a 45-degree fence. Guide the sled on the front edge of the router table. This is a robust bit, but it can't chew a miter in one bite. Saw off the bulk of the waste first.

Molding the full edge

Molding the full edge is like straightening the edge: There's no untouched portion of the edge to guide the cut. The cut requires a separate fence.

Molding the full edge: fence on workpiece

Guide the router base against a fence clamped to the workpiece. Measure the offset to the smallest part of the bit's cutting circle (1), and set the fence that distance from the workpiece edge (2). Rotate the router to put one handle firmly over the contact between base and fence.

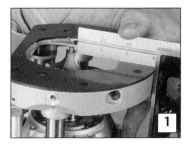

Molding the full edge: router table, split fence

Guide the workpiece against the split fence. Set up the fence as on page 54.

Molding narrow sticks

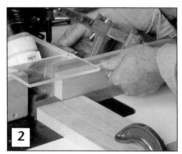

Narrow sticks are liable to chatter and splinter, and they're dangerous to feed. A tunnel stabilizes the setup. One block holds the workpiece in against the fence (1). The other block holds it down (2). Push the strips through the tunnel (3).

Mold the full edge, then rip

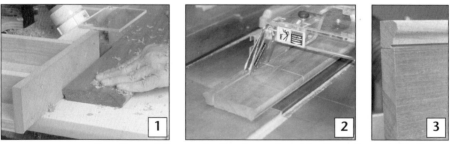

Run the molding on both edges of a wide piece of wood (1), then go to the table saw to rip the moldings from the workpiece (2). Repeat as many times as necessary. This is an economical way to make a molding that stands proud of the surface of the wood (3).

Rebates and moldings

A rebate is a right-angle cutout that leaves a portion of the original edge intact. It is, in fact, an edge molding made with a straight bit instead of a shaped bit. A rebate setup will also work with a molding bit.

Rebates and moldings: pilot bearing

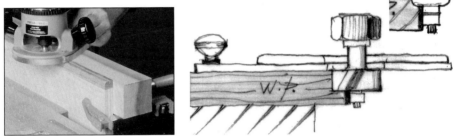

The pilot bearing runs against the uncut portion of the workpiece edge. Clamp the workpiece flat on the bench top, or stand it up on edge in the vise. When the workpiece is up on edge, add an offset base plate and support blocks, as in the photo.

Rebates and moldings: fence on top

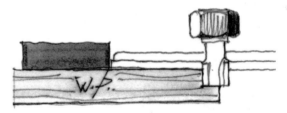

Guide the router base against a straight fence clamped to the workpiece. For moldings, use all or part of the bit profile.

Rebates and moldings: base guide

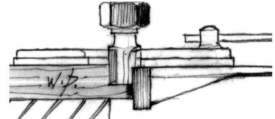

The base guide runs against the uncut portion of the workpiece edge. Clamp the setup overhanging the workbench top.

Rebates and moldings: router table with fence

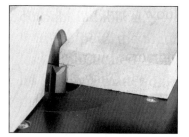

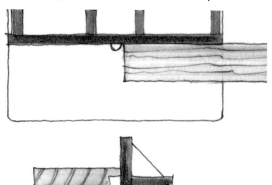

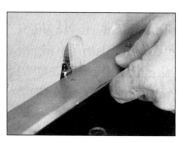

The straight fence supports the uncut portion of the workpiece edge. This is the simplest, most stable, and safest setup. Note that you can use a bit with a pilot bearing, provided you set the fence forward of the bearing surface, as in the photo.

Rebates and moldings: router table, pilot bearing

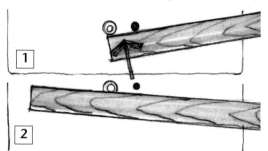

The pilot bearing runs along the uncut portion of the workpiece edge. The starting pin braces the workpiece (1) while you push it onto the bearing. Once the wood is firmly on the bearing, pivot it away from the pin (2) and proceed (page 52).

Rebates and moldings: multiple passes

Moldings like this pencil round take more than one pass across the router table.

Grooves

Grooves run with the grain, while housings (dados) run across the grain (page 140). Make grooves with straight bits or with slot-cutters. Slotting bits have interchangeable cutters and pilot bearings; if the offset from bearing diameter to cutting circle makes too deep a groove, use the straight fence or base guide instead.

Grooving with straight bit

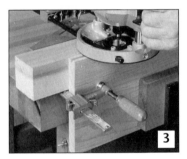

To groove the face of the workpiece, use the base guide (1) or a straight fence (2).

To groove the edge of the workpiece (3), stand it up in the vise, clamp a support rail to it, and use the base guide. You can't accurately groove an edge without a support platform.

Grooving with slot cutter

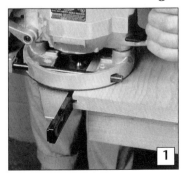
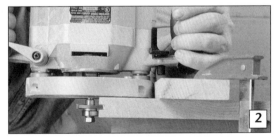

The slot cutter grooves the edge of the workpiece, using the base guide (1) or a straight fence (2).

Grooving with straight bit: router table

Grooving on the router table is simple and safe. A spiral bit gives the best result. Most bits choke the groove with the waste — it's normal. Drag it out with a pencil or an awl.

Grooving with slot cutter: router table

The slot cutter is very efficient. It behaves like a dado cutter in a table saw. It makes a clean and accurate groove.

Grooving the end: router table, high fence

A straight bit can make a groove or slot in the end of the workpiece. Stabilize the wood vertically by clamping it to a support block (1). Keep it tight against the fence by clamping a hold-in to the router table (2).

Grooving the end: router table, sled jig

Cutting end grain *offers more resistance than cutting long grain. The sled takes the uncertainty out of it; a depth stop and a clamp ensure consistent results.*

Groove in mitered end

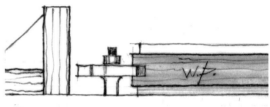

A slot cutter *runs a groove in the mitered end of this frame piece. Clamp the wood to the miter sled (page 125). The fence provides a dust port; it is not involved in the cut.*

Contoured grooves

The semi-circular flutes *in this pilaster start and stop with spot-on accuracy, because of the end stops clamped to the workpiece.*

Housings (dados)

While housings (dados) appear to be the same as grooves, there are two important differences: Housings run across the grain, and in most situations they're nowhere near a useful guide edge. This makes it difficult to set up for housings on the router table. Instead, use the T-square jig (page 111).

Housings (dados): T-square jig

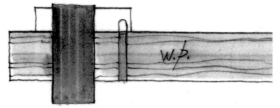

Clamp the T-square jig to the workpiece and guide the router along its edge. Allow the bit to cut into the cross piece, creating an index that shows where the cut will be made (page 111).

Housings (dados): step and repeat

To space housings for shelves in a cabinet, screw a stop block to a spacer and use it to relocate the T-square jig for each cut.

Housings (dados): wider than bit diameter

Rout one side of the housing using the T-square jig. Then turn the jig end-for-end to rout the opposite edge. To rout a lot of housings that are all wider than the diameter of the router bit, it will pay to make up a jig with two fences by joining two T-squares together.

Edge joints

Edge-to-edge joints make the wood wider. Glue is what holds the joint together — rebates, tongues, and splines help align the pieces, but they don't make the joint any stronger than it would be with glue alone.

Tongue and groove

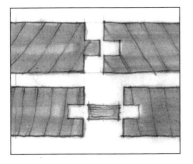

The tongue consists of two rebates, one on each face of the wood (page 135). The groove can be made with a straight bit or with a slot cutter (page 137). The tongue and groove offers no advantage over joining two grooves with a glued spline, and two disadvantages: It wastes wood, and it requires two setups to make.

Spline and groove

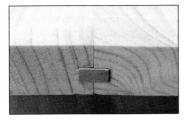

Rout matching grooves in both mating edges. Saw spline stock to fit. The grain of the spline runs the same way as the grain of the wood being joined. While it is possible to rout perfectly centered grooves, there's no advantage. Simply run the face side of both pieces against the router table fence. This ensures that the grooves will line up perfectly, which is all that matters.

Tongue and groove with molding

Make attractive wainscoting by combining a tongue-and-groove or spline-and-groove joint with a decorative molding.

Frame joints

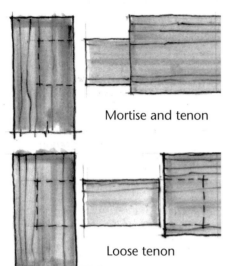

Mortise and tenon

Loose tenon

Frame joints connect two sticks of wood at a right angle. In rectangular frames, the horizontal piece is called the rail and the vertical one is called the stile. Frame joints also connect table aprons and legs, as well as the parts of chairs.

The strongest and most useful frame joint is the mortise and tenon, which comes in many variations. The mortise is the hole, the tenon is the piece that fills the hole. The loose-tenon form of the joint has matching mortises in both frame pieces, bridged by a separate tenon. It's ideal for the router because both parts can be made with one setup.

Frame joints: mortise in edge or in end

The bracket jig is versatile, quick, and stable. It will accept any workpiece and make a mortise of almost any size, on the end, edge or face (page 118).

Frame joints: mortise in square stock

The pocket jig can make matching mortises in adjacent faces of square legs and posts, for chairs, tables, and cabinets. It is quick to set up and reload (page 112).

Frame joints: tenons with saddle jig

Make tenons by routing rebates around the end of the workpiece. The saddle jig (page 114) makes accurate tenons. It requires a guide collar and a straight bit. Tenons with square corners don't fit mortises with round ends. You can pare the mortise square, or radius the square edges of the tenon.

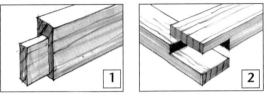

The saddle jig can rout all four shoulders on a tenon (1). A pair of one-faced tenons makes the corner lap joint (2).

Frame joints: loose tenons on router table

To make loose tenons, saw a square-cornered workpiece and rout the corners round, using a roundover bit in the router table. The bit shown has a pilot bearing, but since the cut removes the entire edge, guide it on the fence instead. Make several feet of tenon stock, then saw it to length after routing.

Frame joints: corner bridle

Rout the bridle joint with a straight bit and high fence on the router table. The support blocks are essential to keep the workpiece vertical; the hold-in keeps the workpiece pressed against the fence.

Frame joints: dowels

Glued dowels make strong frame joints, provided the holes are aligned. The bracket jig allows the plunge router to drill extremely accurate dowel holes in the face and end of the workpiece.

Clamp stops to the bracket jig to locate the dowel holes.

Use an up-cutting spiral bit. Drill by plunging the router directly to full depth.

Frame joints: three-way showcase corner

The showcase joint features three identically mortised rails coming together to form a corner. Loose tenons make the connection. More on page 143.

Carcase joints

Carcase joints make corners for boxes and cabinets. The dovetail is the classic corner joint; the box joint is functionally equivalent, but with straight lines instead of angles. You can also make strong boxes using the corner tongue-and-groove.

Carcase joints: dovetail

The router marketplace offers many variations on the dovetail jig, some simple and some quite complex. The Kellar jig shown  here makes a true through dovetail. It's stable, and easy to adjust.

Carcase joints: finger or box

Rout box joints with the step-and-repeat box-joint jig built on a right-angle sled for the router table — see page 126.

Carcase joints: corner tongue and groove

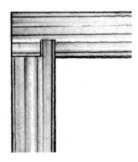

The joint is strongest when the tongue extends from the inside face of the wood. Make the tongue by running a deep rebate from the face of the wood. Make the groove with a straight bit on the router table (page 137).

Raised and fielded panels

Raised and fielded panels are nothing more than moldings run around all four sides of a board. You can raise panels by driving the router over the workpiece, but the process is far less risky on a router table equipped with a high fence.

Raising panels: router on top

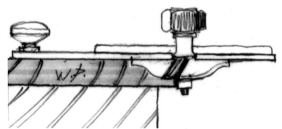

Clamp the setup so it overhangs the edge of the bench. You'll need to reclamp for each edge of the panel.

Raising panels: router table, high fence

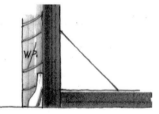

The vertical bit requires standing the workpiece on edge; a high fence stabilizes the setup.

Raising panels: router table, pilot bearing

A panel-raising bit with pilot bearing can be used with a starting pin, as in the photo, or with the straight fence — set the fence flush with or forward of the bearing.

Cope-and-stick

Cope-and-stick is a way of making a molded frame with inside corners that appear to be neatly mitered. The miter is an illusion — the horizontal rail is cut away, or coped, to fit exactly over the molding on the vertical stile.

Cope-and-stick has to be done on the router table, using a matched pair of cutters. Both cutters have a pilot bearing. Along with the stuck molding, the cutters simultaneously make a groove that will retain a panel. Along with the cope, the cutter makes a matching stub tenon on the ends of the rails.

The key to an accurate joint is exactly matching the height of each cutter. Make a set of test cuts before you commit good wood.

Mold the inside edge of all the frame pieces. Use the starting pin and guide the cut on the bearing. The fence provides a top guard and dust exhaust.

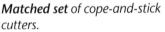

Matched set of cope-and-stick cutters.

To cope the ends of the rails, clamp the workpiece to the right-angle sled (page 124). A stop block clamped to the fence positions the rail ahead of the bearing-guided cutter.

To make the cope, guide the sled along the front edge of the router table.

Pattern-rout parts

The simplest way to reproduce a template or pattern is with a straight bit that has a pilot bearing. When the pilot bearing is the same size as the bit, the part will be a match. When the pilot bearing is larger or smaller, the part will be enlarged or reduced. Remember that the router is a finishing tool, not the best tool for roughing out. Before routing, trace the template onto the blank, and saw the bulk of the waste away.

Pattern rout: template on top

Fasten the pattern to the workpiece with double-stick tape. Clamp the assembly so it overhangs the edge of the bench. Use a straight bit with a shank-mounted bearing, and drive the router around the shape, keeping the bearing pressed against the template.

Pattern rout: router table

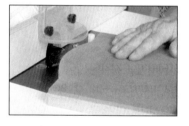

Fasten the pattern to the workpiece with double-stick tape. Use a straight bit with a tip-mounted bearing. Pivot the assembly on the starting pin until the bearing contacts the template, then drive the workpiece around the shape. The table fence provides a top guard and dust port but does not guide the cut.

Pattern rout: router table, sled jig

The jig platform is the template. Trap the workpiece on it with stop blocks and toggle clamps. Use a straight bit with a shank-mounted pilot bearing, begin the cut with the aid of a starting pin (page 123).

Arch-top frame-and-panel doors

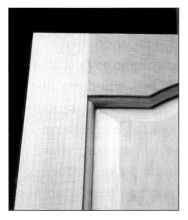

Arch-top paneled doors are popular in kitchens, and the router marketplace offers a number of jig-and-template systems for making them. The elements you need have already been detailed in this catalog: cope-and-stick cutter set for the door frame and corner joint, pattern-routing sled jig for the shaped top rail, panel template and horizontal panel-raising bit.

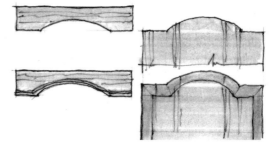

Shape the panel on the router table by following a top-mounted template (page 148).

Raise the panel with a horizontal bit. The pilot bearing rides the shaped edge of the workpiece (page 146).

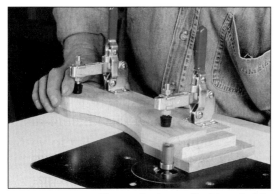

Shape the top rail with a sled jig on the router table (page 148).

Rout the joints, and mold the inside edge of the frame, with a cope-and-stick cutter set on the router table (page 147).

Index

Index

Photographs:	John Kelsey
Drawings:	Ian Kirby
Photo scans:	Morgan Kelsey
Text editor:	Joe Henry
Groaning:	Dag Nabbit
Paper:	Silverado Matte
Typeface:	Stone serif, sans and informal
Manufacturing:	Vaughan Printing, Nashville TN